# STORYTELLING:
## ART AND TECHNIQUE

# STORYTELLING:

## ART AND TECHNIQUE

### SECOND EDITION

**by Augusta Baker
and Ellin Greene**

**R. R. BOWKER COMPANY**
NEW YORK & LONDON, 1987

Published by R. R. Bowker Company,
a division of Reed Publishing (USA) Inc.
Copyright © 1987 by Augusta Baker and Ellin Greene
All rights reserved
Printed and bound in the United States of America

**Library of Congress Cataloging-in-Publication Data**

Baker, Augusta.
   Storytelling : art and technique / by Augusta Baker and Ellin
Greene. — 2nd ed.
        p.    cm.
   Bibliography: p.
   Includes index.
   ISBN 0-8352-2336-1
   1. Storytelling—United States.     I. Greene, Ellin, 1927–
II. Title.   III. Title: Story telling.
LB1042.B34   1987
808.06'8543—dc 19                                    87-26539
                                                       CIP

Dedicated
to
Mary Gould Davis

# Contents

# Preface

The art and practice of storytelling has flourished in the United States during the decade following the publication of the first edition of *Storytelling: Art and Technique* (1977). The growth of storytelling organizations at the national, regional, state, and local levels (in particular, the National Association for the Preservation and Perpetuation of Storytelling), and the emergence of the professional storyteller-entertainer, has brought storytelling to coffeehouses, theaters, concert halls, and festivals across the country as well as to more traditional settings. Public libraries have extended their storytelling programs to infants and toddlers and their caregivers while decreasing the number of story hours for the middle age group, that is, children between the ages of 8 and 11. A shortage of children's librarians and recent research that demonstrated the relationship between sharing stories aloud with the very young child and language acquisition, motivation to read, and cognitive/emotional development provided the rationale for this reordering of priorities.

But storytelling has much to offer older children and young adolescents. In communities where other activities compete for the older child's attention and formal story hours do not attract these children, librarians have discovered that these youngsters enjoy learning and practicing the art of storytelling themselves.

The second edition of *Storytelling: Art and Technique* has been written in response to the many requests for further information and updated bibliographies. We have kept the format of the previous edition—"a manual in the best possible sense"—in order to make the information readily available. We have added a section on storytelling to infants and toddlers (Chapter 6), a chapter on children and young adults as storytellers (Chapter 7), and expanded and updated the bibliographies.

Our book is designed to meet the special needs of the librarian/teacher-storyteller, but professional storytellers who practice in a school or library setting, recreation leaders, child caregivers, and other adults interested in the art of storytelling will also find *Storytelling: Art and Technique* helpful. Our goal is to instill confidence in librarians and teachers as storytellers so that they will share stories with children on a *regular* basis.

Our emphasis throughout is on storytelling as an oral art. We believe that storytelling as a listening/language experience should not be lost. Our eye-minded society has forgotten the power of the spoken word and emphasizes the visual, reducing written language to everyday speech, but in storytelling the full range of language is possible. Aidan Chalmers, in his book *Introducing Books to Children* (Boston: Horn Book, 1983, p. 130) writes:

> As children listen to stories, verse, prose of all kinds, they unconsciously become familiar with the rhythms and structure, the cadences and conventions of the various forms of written language. They are learning how print "sounds," how to "hear" it in their inner ear. Only through listening to words in print being spoken does anyone discover their color, their life, their movement and drama.

Storytelling at its best is mutual creation. Children listen and, out of the words they hear, create their own mental images; this opening of the mind's eye develops the imagination. Many contemporary storytellers, in an effort to compete successfully with television and the visual arts, have turned away from the oral tradition, with the result that storytelling, particularly for younger children, is often limited to the sharing of picture books. As beautiful as picture-book art is (and we do not wish to detract from its value), we feel that listening can be a complete experience, even for young children.

Through the stories themselves and through the interaction between teller and listener, traditional storytelling goes beyond the surface child to speak to the inner child. Storytelling activities, such as flannel-board stories, costumes, and gimmicks, may entertain children, but they do not necessarily recreate the human spirit. We are more concerned with touching this inner child, with nurturing the spirit-self, and with enriching and deepening a child's feelings, than with entertainment.

We have tried to bring together the most successful methods of storytelling by master storytellers. Chapter 1 consists of a brief history of storytelling in libraries in the United States and short biographical sketches of some of the early storytellers who gave impetus to the growth of storytelling in libraries, schools, and recreation centers during the first half of the twentieth century. Well-known living storytellers have not been included. Much of the material in this first chapter is based on unpublished manuscripts and papers from the files of the Office of Children's Services, The New York Public Library, with which both authors have been closely associated.

Chapter 2 restates the purpose and values of storytelling. Storytelling is an art, and as such needs no justification. Unfortunately, teachers sometimes find themselves in positions where they must defend the inclusion of storytelling in their work to skeptical administrators, colleagues, or the community's educational leaders. Awareness of the educational values of storytelling will give new storytellers a sound basis for sharing stories with children in the classroom.

Succeeding chapters cover the types of literature (both traditional and modern) that lend themselves to storytelling, the principles of selection, basic techniques (preparation and presentation) of learning and telling a story, program planning (with sample programs), the administration of storytelling programs, and in-service courses in storytelling. Suggestions are also included for storytelling in special settings, such as parks, playgrounds, camps, and hospitals, and to groups with special needs.

We have paid particular attention to selection because most librarians, teachers, and recreation leaders, unlike folklorists, who gather their material directly from oral sources, are dependent on the printed word for their storytelling material. We believe, therefore, that selecting the right story out of the vast body of literature available today is one of the most important aspects of storytelling.

The questions scattered throughout the text are those most frequently asked by participants in workshops we conducted in school and public libraries and colleges throughout the United States over the past 20 years.

An extensive bibliography includes books on the art of storytelling, collections and single editions of storytelling literature, storytelling recordings, and stories to tell children at various age levels. Most of these stories have been favorites of children over a long period of time, and all of them have qualities that make them easy to tell. Titles of books now out of print, but too good to miss, are included because they still can be found in libraries and secondhand bookstores. Annotations are given for titles that do not clearly indicate the contents.

Because our basic concern is with the *told* story, we have not included techniques for picture-book storytelling. Picture-books are listed in the bibliographies because they are a source for the storyteller and the illustrations are an aid to learning the story. Where the text is extensive, we suggest that the tale first be told without the pictures; then the illustrations can be shared with the children. For the same reason, we have not covered penny theater, puppetry, creative dramatics, and storytelling through movement and dance. Each of these art forms merits separate attention.

The authors gratefully acknowledge the assistance of their editors, Marion Sader, Executive Editor; Olga S. Weber and Julia Raymunt, Managing Editors, and Iris Topel, Editing Supervisor, in the preparation of this manual; and Lynette Reed in typing the manuscript. We are indebted to the staffs of the Office of Children's Services and the Central Children's Room, The New York Public Library, for their assistance in locating materials and verifying dates. We also wish to thank Carol Birch for choreographing a section of "The Wooing of the Maze." Lastly, we would be remiss if we did not thank our fellow storytellers and students for their encouragement, advice, and inspiration.

Augusta Baker
Ellin Greene

# Acknowledgments

The authors wish to thank the following publishers for permission to quote material from their books and journals: Atheneum Publishers, Inc., for excerpts from *The Rat-Catcher's Daughter: Stories by Laurence Housman*, selected and with an afterword by Ellin Greene. Copyright © 1974 by Atheneum Publishers. Used by permission of Atheneum Publishers; Cambridge University Press for an excerpt from *The Ordinary and the Fabulous* by Elizabeth Cook. Copyright © 1976 Cambridge University Press. Used by permission; Jonathan Cape, Ltd., and the Executors of the Laurence Housman Estate for excerpts from "The Rat-Catcher's Daughter" and "The Wooing of the Maze" from *Doorway in Fairyland* by Laurence Housman; *Catholic Library World* for an excerpt from "The Art of Storytelling" by Elizabeth Nesbitt, reprinted from *Catholic Library World*, November 1962; The Dial Press for an excerpt from *The Knee-High Man and Other Tales* by Julius Lester. Copyright © 1972 by Julius Lester. Reprinted by permission of The Dial Press; Grosset and Dunlap, Inc., for an excerpt from *Favorite Fairy Tales to Read Aloud*. Copyright © 1958 by Wonder Books, Inc. Used by permission of Grosset & Dunlap, Inc.; Harcourt Brace Jovanovich, Inc., for excerpts from *Rootabaga Stories* by Carl Sandburg. Reprinted by permission of Harcourt Brace Jovanovich, Inc.; Heinemann Educational Books, Ltd., for an excerpt from *Introducing Books to Children* by Aidan Chalmers. Reprinted by permission of Heinemann Educational Books and The Horn Book, Inc., © 1973, 1983 by Aidan Chalmers; Heritage Press for an excerpt from *The Complete Andersen: A Collection of 168 Fairy Tales by Hans Christian Andersen*, translated by Jean Hersholt. Copyright © 1977 by Heritage Press; Holt, Rinehart and Winston Publishers for an excerpt from *Heather and Broom: Tales of the Scottish Highlands* by Sorche Nic Leodhas. Copyright © 1960 by Leclaire G. Alger. Reprinted by permission of Holt, Rinehart and Winston Publishers and McIntosh and Otis, Inc.; The Horn Book, Inc., for excerpts from *My Roads to Childhood* by Anne Carroll Moore. Copyright © 1961 by The Horn Book, Inc.; *The Horn Book Magazine* for an excerpt from "Hold to That Which Is Good" by Elizabeth Nesbitt, reprinted from *The Horn Book Magazine*, January/February 1940. Copyright © by The Horn Book, Inc.; *The Horn Book Magazine* for an excerpt from "The Pleasant Land of Counterpane" by Claudia Lewis, reprinted from *The Horn Book Magazine*, October 1966. Copyright © by The Horn Book, Inc.; Alfred A. Knopf, Inc., for an excerpt from *The Uses of Enchantment: The Meaning and Importance of Fairy Tales* by Bruno Bettelheim. Copyright © 1976 by Bruno Bettelheim. Portions of this book originally appeared in *The New Yorker.* Reprinted by permission of Alfred A. Knopf, Inc.; Mrs. Robert A. Leflar for an excerpt from "The Magic Ball" in *Tales from Silver Lands* by Charles J. Finger (1925 Newbery Award winner); these articles first appeared in *National Storytelling Journal* and are reprinted with the permission of Carol L. Birch and Kay Stone: Carol L. Birch, "Storytelling Programs for the Family," *National Storytelling Journal*, Summer 1984, p. 17, and Kay Stone, "'To Ease the Heart': Traditional Storytelling," *National Storytelling Journal*, Winter 1984, p. 5. The New York Public Library for an excerpt from Ruth Sawyer's "Storytelling: Fifty Years A-growing" in *Reading without Boundaries*, edited by Frances Lander Spain. Copyright © 1956 by The New York Public Library; Harold Ober Associates, Inc., for an excerpt from *Martin Pippin in the Daisy Field* by Eleanor Farjeon. Copyright © 1937 by Eleanor Farjeon. Renewed. Reprinted by permission of Harold Ober Associates, Inc.; Pantheon Books, a division of Random House, Inc., for an excerpt from Padraic Colum's introduction to *The Complete Grimm's Fairy Tales* by Jakob Karl Grimm and Wilhelm Karl Grimm, translated by Margaret Hunt and James Stern. Copyright © 1944 by Pantheon Books, Inc., and renewed 1972 by Random House, Inc. Reprinted by permission of Pantheon Books, a division of Random House, Inc.; *Top of the News* for an excerpt from "Recorded Magic for Story Hours" by Spencer Shaw in *Top of the News*, October 1958; University of Chicago Press for an excerpt from *The Panchatantra*, translated by Arthur W. Ryder. Copyright © 1925 by University of Chicago Press. Reprinted by permission of the University of Chicago Press; The Viking Press, Inc., for an excerpt from *Journey to the People* by Ann Nolan Clark. Copyright © 1969 by Ann Nolan Clark. Reprinted by permission of The Viking Press, Inc.; Verna Aardema Vugteveen for an excerpt from *Tales for the Third Ear: From Equatorial Africa* by Verna Aardema. Copyright © 1969 by Verna Aardema;

Frederick Warne & Co., Inc., for an excerpt from *The Golden Goose Book* by L. Leslie Brooke. Used by permission of Frederick Warne & Co., Inc.; from Howard Gardner, *The Arts and Human Development*, © 1973 by John Wiley & Sons, used with permission; The H. W. Wilson Company for an excerpt from *Let's Listen to a Story* by Lilian Okun. Copyright © 1959 by Lilian Okun; *Wilson Library Bulletin* for an excerpt from "A Story Falls in the Silence" by Spencer G. Shaw, reprinted from the *Wilson Library Bulletin*, October 1964. Copyright © 1964 by The H. W. Wilson Company.

# 1 Background

Whoever knows the book by heart
Or through the storyteller's art
Becomes acquainted,
His life by sad defeat—although
The King of Heaven be his foe—
Is never tainted.
    —*The Panchatantra*[1]

Storytelling is older than history and is not bounded by one civilization, one continent, or one race. Stories differ from place to place; the purposes and conditions of storytelling change as we move from century to century; and yet, in all the different lands and periods of time, storytelling has filled the same basic social and individual needs. Curiosity about the past, the search for an understanding of beginnings, the need for entertainment, and the desire to keep alive a heroic past established the early storyteller as bringer of news, historian, disperser of culture, upholder of religion and morals, as well as entertainer. As time went on, the stories became a mixture of legends, mythology, hero tales, and anonymous personal tales, and the storyteller became an important, respected member of the community. Men and women hung upon the storytellers' words and listened eagerly to the tales.

In Africa there were the "resident storyteller" and the "traveling storyteller." The former was part of a chief's household and had only the responsibility of keeping alive the exploits of this leader. The "traveling storyteller," however, went from village to village with tales, anecdotes, and fables and became the collector of an oral, narrative tradition. In Japan, China, and India the scholar, the priest, the artisan, and the peasant were greatly respected as storytellers.

In other parts of the world the art of storytelling had long existed. The first written record of an activity that appears to be storytelling is found in an Egyptian papyrus called the Westcar Papyrus and tells how the sons of Cheops, the famous builder of pyramids, entertained their father with stories. Those tales were recorded sometime between 2000 and 1300 B.C.

The earliest known heroic epic, *Gilgamesh*, was first told by the Sumerians, the inventors of the written word, and was taken over by the Babylonians when the Sumerian civilization collapsed in 2000 B.C. The great epics of *Beowulf* and the Finnish *Kalevala* were told for centuries before they were recorded by scholars. The Greek myths, told by storytellers, explained the creation of the world and the terrifying forces of nature. These storytellers created supernatural beings with the power to rule such forces, and yet these gods had human frailties.

Anglo-Saxon "gleemen" and, later, Norman minstrels sang their stories. They traveled all over England and the Continent learning new tales and passing them on in song, dance, and story. These minstrels were found in many countries: in Germany there were the minnesingers, members of the music and poetry guilds; in Ireland, the ollams, known as master storytellers, and the shanachies, who told their stories by the glow of the peat fires.

Scholars began to write down these stories and, with the invention of printing in 1450, the minstrel tradition of storytelling began to wane. Though music and poetry remained, the traditional prose tale, the story handed down from generation to generation either in writing or by word of mouth, became the stuff of storytelling.

Folklorists began to search out and preserve these tales, and soon the collecting of oral narrative forms became an important part of the oral tradition. Out of this work came the great written collections of the Brothers Grimm, Alexander Afanasiev, Joseph Jacobs, Peter Asbjørnsen and Jørgen Moe, Jeremiah Curtin, Joseph Campbell, and others. Attempts were made to preserve tradition and the authority of antiquity and to give the stories interest and importance.

Though books appeared, the storytelling tradition endured, so that today these same prose tales are told over and over again in various parts of the world. And the long, complex interplay of oral tradition and written literature continues.

Important as these early poets, troubadours, wandering minstrels, and storytellers were, they have not been solely responsible for keeping alive the hundreds of old tales we enjoy today. Parents, grandparents, nannies, and other child caregivers have always told stories to amuse children. Rare was the family that did not have some member to tell stories over and over again around the fireplace or when the children were tucked into bed.

The first organized program of storytelling to children took place in kindergartens. When the German educator Friedrich Froebel founded the kindergarten movement in 1837, he made storytelling an important part of the curriculum. German emigrants to America took with them the idea of kindergartens, and in 1873 the first kindergarten was incorporated into a public school system in the United States. Instruction in storytelling was given in the kindergarten training schools, and in 1905 Sara Cone Bryant, a kindergarten teacher, wrote the first storytelling text to be published in the United States, *How to Tell Stories to Children* (Houghton).

The playground movement and the growth of settlement houses also encouraged storytelling to children. Then came story hours in libraries. It was a logical development of the long history of the art. Children's libraries and the first "department for work with children" were formed in the late nineteenth century. Librarians were seeking ways to bring together children and books and to interpret literature in an artistic rather than in a didactic manner.

The exact date of the first library story hour is uncertain, but it was about 1900. As early as 1896 Anne Carroll Moore had given storytelling a place in the children's room of the new Pratt Institute Free Library in Brooklyn, New York. Storytelling had been tried experimentally as early as 1899 in the Carnegie Library of Pittsburgh, just a year after the organization of the department for work with children. Storytelling had such spectacular success that Frances Jenkins Olcott, who was the director of children's work, incorporated the story hour as a regular part of the program. In the same year the Buffalo Public Library started regular Saturday morning story hours, having already experimented the year before with storytelling on Sunday afternoons to stimulate interest in books and reading.

Similar experiments were being carried out in other newly organized children's rooms, and children's librarians were beginning to recognize the great potential of storytelling when, in 1900, Marie Shedlock came to the United States to lecture on Hans Christian Andersen and to tell her fairy tales to children and adults.

## Marie Shedlock

Marie Shedlock, with a background of many years of teaching, became a professional storyteller in London about 1890. Her lectures to teachers became the basis for a book that is still a classic in storytelling, *The Art of the Story-teller* (Dover). She lectured in France as well as in England, but her real success came in the United States, where she gave library storytelling the impetus it needed.

It was on Marie Shedlock's first visit to the United States that Mary Wright Plummer, director of the School of Library Science at Pratt Institute in Brooklyn, heard her tell stories in French and English at one of a series of matinees at Sherry's, a fashionable New York City restaurant of the day. She told Hans Christian Andersen's "Tin Soldier," "The Swineherd," and "The Princess and the Pea," and the telling was unforgettable. When Andersen died, it was said that his fairy tales would live forever in the hearts of children, but Mary Wright Plummer thought that these stories should live in the minds of children, too. Mary Wright Plummer invited Marie Shedlock to tell her stories to the trustees, directors, and faculty of Pratt Institute Free Library. Anne Carroll Moore, the children's librarian, was one of those who heard her tell Laurence Housman's "A Chinese Fairy Tale," or "Tikipu," as she called it, that day.

It was customary for storytellers at that time to use the affected speech and gestures of elocution. The stories themselves were often filled with didactic material. Marie Shedlock, however, was a true artist, sharing great literature. This was real storytelling! Anne Carroll Moore decided that there must be a story hour for the children, too, and so, one Saturday morning, the children listened to Marie Shedlock and were enthralled. So impressed was one small child that afterwards she asked in wonder, "Is she a fairy or just a lady?" Anne Carroll Moore wrote in later years,

"There was never any doubt in my mind after that morning that a children's library should have a regular story hour."[2]

Though story hours were being conducted in some library systems before Marie Shedlock came to the United States, it was her inspiration, as she traveled throughout the country, telling stories, lecturing, and training storytellers, that gave impetus to the idea of storytelling as a true art. She visited Boston, Chicago, the Pacific Coast, and other places, giving practical instruction in the art of storytelling and emphasizing the importance of selecting out of great literature stories little known or long forgotten. After her visit to Boston in 1902, regular library story hours were established. By 1911 the Boston Public Library had employed Mary W. Cronan to hold weekly story hours in one of the branches. Later the storytellers were increased to three with special training—Mary Cronan, her husband, John Cronan, and her sister, Margaret Powers. In 1953, the Cronans were still telling hero tales to groups of Boston children.[3]

In Pittsburgh, too, storytelling assumed a new importance in these years. Pittsburgh librarians began to take stories to the playgrounds and to hold weekly story hours in their branches. By 1909 Edna Whiteman was appointed supervisor of storytelling. She selected versions of stories most suitable for telling, arranged programs, and told stories in the children's rooms of library branches. In 1916 she prepared the first edition of *Stories to Tell to Children: A Selected List*, which is now in its eighth revised edition.

In the Cleveland Public Library, Carolyn Burnite, who took over the organization of work with children in 1904, established storytelling as an important, regular part of the work. Usually two story hours a week were held in each branch library. Because storytelling was regarded as one of the children's librarian's responsibilities, time was allowed for the preparation of stories. As time went on, more and more children came to hear the stories until, in 1909, the total number of children who attended story hours was 80,996.[4]

At the same time the Chicago Public Library was using the talent of an outstanding storyteller, Gudrun Thorne-Thomsen, who was also telling stories in the field houses of the public recreation centers. Private organizations supported the storytelling movement financially, and both the director of playgrounds and the chief librarian of the Chicago Public Library strongly favored it. The chief librarian, Henry L. Legler, was quoted as saying in 1910: "We are now engaged in developing the branch library system of the city and no doubt storytelling will be made incidentally a feature of the work planned for children's rooms. This work must be done by the children's librarians, the storytelling growing out of library work and merging into it in order that its most effective side be legitimately developed."[5]

Anne Carroll Moore, at the Pratt Institute Free Library in Brooklyn, had not rushed to select her first storyteller even though she was convinced that there should be a regular story hour. She wrote in later years:

> Finding a story-teller of the right sort was not easy. Poor story-telling is more disastrous than poor story-writing, which can be skipped or left entirely alone without affecting anyone else. I had been conscious from the first months of my personal work in a children's room of the need for investing reading with dramatic interest and pictorial tradition, if it were to have any real meaning in the daily lives of hundreds of children who were coming to the library. . . .[6]

For a year after Marie Shedlock's visit to Brooklyn, Anne Carroll Moore conducted an experimental story hour, inviting different people to tell stories as she and the children listened. She described one memorable story hour in her book *My Roads to Childhood:*

> I learned a very great deal from listening. In the spring of that year Miss Shedlock came back again and told Hans Christian Andersen's "Nightingale." It woke the story-teller for whom I had been waiting so long, and on May Eve, a Robin Hood story from Howard Pyle and a true story out of her own childhood marked the first of Anna Cogswell Tyler's distinctive contributions to story-telling.[7]

## Anna Cogswell Tyler

Anna Cogswell Tyler, Anne Carroll Moore's young assistant, had heard Marie Shedlock tell stories to the boys and girls of Brooklyn on that exciting Saturday morning. Anna Tyler had had dramatic training but, bowing to family pressures, she did not go on the stage. Storytelling, however, was the answer to this dramatic urge. In 1907, a year after Anne Carroll Moore's appointment as the first supervisor of work with children at the New York Public Library, she brought Anna Tyler to the library to develop a storytelling program. By 1909 a strong storytelling program was in progress and Anna Tyler had been appointed the first supervisor of storytelling for the library. In a 1909 report she wrote:

> We are striving to make a more direct application between the story told and the book itself. This we do by only telling stories that will interest the children in the special book from which the story is told. . . . The Assistant in Charge of Storytelling is giving more careful supervision to all those assistants telling stories in the libraries; helping in the choice of story, selecting the best versions to use, directing as far as possible their advance reading, and generally trying to so mould the work of the storyhour that it may assume a more definite, lasting and literary form, while trying in each case to fit the particular needs and interests of the children. Already the storyhour has assumed a more dignified and definite aspect both in the kinds of stories told and the manner in which the storyhour is being conducted. Each month the storyhour is fast losing its haphazard appearance and is entering upon its proper function in library economy—that of introducing children to the best kind of books, arousing a desire for a wider range in reading in boys and girls who, having fallen into the clutches of the series habit, seem unable to be interested in anything outside that rut until they listen to a well-told story of a great deed or a great romance, handle the book which contains it, learn to know where it may be found, and, the interest once aroused, the book is in constant demand.[8]

In 1909, the storytelling staff told stories to 28,325 children; in 1910, 1,008 story hours were held for 30,000 children in 36 libraries. Anna Tyler planned and held staff workshops, gave on-the-job training, and inspired the new storytellers with her own art. She knew the need for inspiration, and so she held the first Spring Storytelling Symposium in 1909, where fledgling storytellers could by the example of their own art inspire others to become storytellers. One of her innovative ideas was a weekly evening story hour for nonreading boys that was held in a branch library during the months November 1909 to May 1910. The boys' interest in books was stimulated, and the books used in the story hours began to circulate.

Anna Cogswell Tyler's influence spread throughout the profession as she held workshops and chaired storytelling committees for the Playground Association of America, Clark University, New York City's Board of Education, and others. In 1921 she compiled her favorite stories in *Twenty-four Unusual Stories* (Harcourt). On her retirement in 1922 she was succeeded as supervisor of storytelling by her young assistant, Mary Gould Davis.

## Mary Gould Davis

Mary Gould Davis was born in Bangor, Maine, on February 13, 1882, the seventh of eight children. Shortly thereafter, the family moved to the Cumberland Mountains of Kentucky, and though they finally settled in New York in 1896, Miss Davis never lost her love for Kentucky and the mountain folk. Every night her mother read to the children, or their Irish nurse, Mary, told them stories. It was a book-loving family, and half a century later Mary Gould Davis still shared these stories and poems with boys and girls. According to Mary Gould Davis, she had a "haphazard education" under the guidance of a governess and in private schools and then began her career in the Brooklyn Public Library. In 1910 she went to the New York Public Library, where she became an assistant to Anna Cogswell Tyler, whom she succeeded in 1922 as supervisor of storytelling.

The new supervisor believed that only training and experience can make storytelling effective and that a controlled story hour encouraged the children to listen with a deep quietness, and so New York Public Library story hours, under her direction, were formal and dignified, with fresh flowers, a wishing candle, and books on the table. The story-hour line, the well-planned program, careful selection of stories—all were part of Mary Gould Davis's philosophy. An adult who heard her tell stories during this period described her telling and the children's reactions to her:

> For them she changed these stories from being something with which you kept children quiet at the end of the day into something they must have, a part of their heritage of wonder and laughter, of

understanding, of perception. The telling of a tale deserved the creative effort and discipline which a work of art demands. I have often wished I could draw adequately the faces of one of the audiences. Over all of them, young and old, passed each emotion evoked by the tale—awe, solemnity, suspense, and the quick flicker of humor. Her voice was gifted, her timing perfect, her gestures controlled. There was never anything histrionic, for a story was never a medium for her own virtuosity, but her consummate skill was the medium for her story. "That Foolish Mr. Bun," "The Timid Little Hare," "Molly Whuppie" have been passed on with as vivid and distinct personalities as those of people we know well.[9]

Beginning in 1923 Mary Gould Davis found time to travel abroad—to England, Italy, Spain, the Island of Skye in Scotland—to search out stories and to trace versions of those she already knew. *Truce of the Wolf* (Harcourt) was her collection of tales from Tuscany and Umbria, and *Three Golden Oranges and Other Spanish Folk Tales*, with Ralph Boggs (Longmans), was a collection of stories from Spain. In 1945 she collaborated with Ernest Kalibala in *Wakaima and the Clay Man* (Longmans), a collection of East African folktales. She wrote a short biography of Randolph Caldecott, which was published on the occasion of the one hundredth anniversary of his birth, prepared new editions of the Andrew Lang "color" fairy-tale books, and contributed to many periodicals and encyclopedias. For several years she was editor of a department of the *Saturday Review of Literature*, "Books for Young People." From the classes she taught at the School of Library Service, Columbia University, storytellers carried her philosophy across the country and to foreign lands. Mary Gould Davis retired from the New York Public Library in 1945 and died in April 1956.

One day of the Miami Beach Storytelling Festival at the American Library Association Conference, held in June 1956, was dedicated to Mary Gould Davis, and admiring librarians told stories there in her honor. (Figure 1.)

Another storyteller who was honored at the festival was Ruth Sawyer.

## Ruth Sawyer

At Christmastime in 1910 the opportunity that Ruth Sawyer had been waiting for finally presented itself. A storyteller was needed for the Christmas story hour at the Hudson Park Branch

**MARY GOULD DAVIS DAY**

**Tuesday, June 19, 1956**

THE GOAT WELL

Source: *The Fire on the Mountain*
By Harold Courlander and Wolf
Leslau. Holt. 1950

MRS. AUGUSTA BAKER

* * *

THE PEDDLER OF BALLAGHADEREEN

Source: *The Way of the Storyteller*
By Ruth Sawyer
Viking. 1942

MARJORIE DOBSON

* * *

THE OLD MAN OF THE FLOWERS

Source: *The Dancing Kettle*
By Yoshiko Uchida
Harcourt, Brace. 1949
(Told in Japanese)

SHIGEO WATANABE

* * *

THE NIGHTINGALE, BY HANS C. ANDERSEN

Source: *The Art of the Story-Teller*
By Marie L. Shedlock
Third edition, revised
Dover. 1951

MARY STRANG

FIGURE 1. Program for a storytelling festival presented by the Children's Library Association at the ALA Miami Beach Conference on June 19, 1956. This day was dedicated to Mary Gould Davis.

of the New York Public Library, and Anne Carroll Moore had invited her to fill the gap. She accepted with pleasure.

The story Ruth Sawyer told at this, her first library story hour, was "The Voyage of the Wee Red Cap," and it became thereafter a part of the Christmas tradition of the New York Public Library. Rarely did Ruth Sawyer miss the St. Nicholas Eve program, and rarely did she miss telling one of her Christmas stories. "Rich in feeling for Christmas, gifted with a beautiful singing voice, clear memory, keen sense of humor, faith in the unseen, and indomitable personal courage and capacity to share the interests of others, she has been able to give dramatic joy to thousands of as strangely assorted people as ever came together upon this earth," Anne Carroll Moore remembered later.[10]

Ruth Sawyer was born in Boston in 1880 but grew up in New York City where she was educated in private schools and in the Garland Kindergarten Training School. Her introduction to storytelling came from her Irish nurse, Johanna, who instilled in her a deep love of Irish folklore. She herself began telling stories and collecting folklore when she was sent to Cuba in 1900 to organize kindergartens. At Columbia University, where she had been awarded a scholarship, she studied folklore. She began to tell stories in schools, and then came the memorable experience of hearing Marie Shedlock tell Andersen fairy tales. "It was Miss Shedlock who lighted the fuse that shot me into storytelling in earnest," she wrote.[11]

Ruth Sawyer's opportunity to delve seriously into the sources of folktales came first in 1905 and again in 1907 when the *New York Sun* sent her to Ireland to write a series of articles on Irish cottage industries, Irish folklore, and Gaelic festivals. During this trip, she heard what became perhaps her best-known story, "The Voyage of the Wee Red Cap."

Upon her return to New York City, she spent a winter telling stories from one end of the city to another. She went to nearby states and later wrote:

> One of the best of my storytelling experiences was at the Boys' Club in Greenwich, Connecticut. There were about eighty boys in the club, confirmed crapshooters, pool-players and delinquents. I held them for the first three days by telling them stories of the Ringling Brothers Circus and the few days I had been travelling with it. From

the circus we passed on to Kipling, Stockton, Mark Twain, and the boys started using the library.[12]

Later Ruth Sawyer went to Spain, and the stories she heard and retold were included in *Picture Tales from Spain* (Stokes). Out of this experience, too, came *Tonio Antonio* (Viking). In Mexico she found material for *The Least One* (Viking). She collected Christmas stories from around the world and brought them together in *The Long Christmas* (Viking). *The Way of the Storyteller* (Viking), a book about storytelling as a creative art that should be familiar to all storytellers, and *My Spain*, a "storyteller's year of collecting," followed.

Ruth Sawyer was awarded the Newbery Medal in 1937 for *Roller Skates* (Viking), a story based on her childhood experiences in New York City, and the Regina Medal in 1965 for "a lifetime of distinguished contribution to children's literature." That same year she received the Laura Ingalls Wilder Award from the Children's Services Division (now the Association for Library Service to Children), American Library Association, for books that "over a period of years have made a substantial and lasting contribution to literature for children."

Ruth Sawyer's acceptance of this award was a memorable occasion for the many storytellers who saw her stand before the large audience, a frail woman of 85 years, and with a deep and resonant voice begin, "Once upon a time."

The beautiful voice was stilled forever when Ruth Sawyer died in 1970. Beryl Robinson, a Boston Public Library storyteller who had heard her often, wrote this remembrance of her:

> Ruth Sawyer's life brought rich gifts to children everywhere. Gifts of fun and laughter and wonder. Of thoughtfulness, deep absorption, and joy. Gifts that inspire courage and bring awareness of beauty. The stretching of the imagination, the opening of the heart, and the widening of the horizons that come whenever there is good storytelling, whether given richly by the master storyteller or read from a beautifully written page. But she was also a great teacher; and countless numbers of children in the future will share in her giving as their teachers and librarians follow the way of the storyteller she so brilliantly illumined for them.[13]

## Gudrun Thorne-Thomsen

In 1944 a group of children's librarians listened to a small, quiet, unassuming woman tell "East of the Sun and West of the Moon." The story came alive as this master storyteller used only her lovely voice, perfect timing, and unobtrusive, spontaneous gestures to tell the tale. These librarians were so inspired by Gudrun Thorne-Thomsen that they returned to the children's rooms of the New York Public Library more determined than ever to bring stories to their children and to be the best storytellers possible.

Gudrun Thorne-Thomsen was born on April 8, 1873, in Trondheim, located on one of Norway's beautiful fjords and famous for its great cathedral. When she was 4 years old the family moved to Bergen, Norway's chief seaport, where she saw ships of many countries and listened to the sailors' tales from other lands. Her grandmother read to her and to the other children in the family and told them stories about the great Norse heroes and about trolls and nissen.

Gudrun's mother was Fredrikke Nielsen, a well-loved actress in the Bergen National Theatre and a foremost interpreter of Ibsen. The home Gudrun grew up in was an exciting place, frequented by famous musicians, poets, and writers and alive with amateur theatricals, singing, and storytelling, in which the entire family took part. It is little wonder, then, that Gudrun grew to love literature, to understand the strength and power of words, and to scorn careless speech.

In 1888, when Gudrun was 15 years old, she came to Chicago to live with her older sister. There she trained to be a teacher at the Cook County Normal School and came under the influence of Colonel Francis W. Parker, "the father of progressive education." In 1893, Gudrun married Georg Thorne-Thomsen. The young couple made their home in Chicago and Gudrun joined the staff of Parker's new school. Parker's innovative ideas in education attracted the attention of William Rainey Harper, then president of the University of Chicago. Harper invited Parker to bring his school to the university as part of the newly formed School of Education and to become director of the Laboratory Elementary School. John Dewey, already at the university as head of the Elementary School of the Department of Pedagogy, was appointed head of the Laboratory High School. The Laboratory Schools were Froebel-inspired, and storytelling was prominent in the curriculum. Harper, active in the Chautauqua movement and a storyteller himself, strongly supported the appointment of Gudrun Thorne-Thomsen to the faculty of the university as critic teacher, third grade of the Elementary School, and instructor in the School of Education, in 1901. She taught courses in oral reading, history and literature for lower grades, reading in primary grades, children's literature, and storytelling. Gudrun Thorne-Thomsen believed that listening to oral literature prepared children for reading. She recommended that teachers turn to storytelling when children became stuck in decoding. She began retelling the old Norse folktales for children, and out of this came her first book, *East of the Sun and West of the Moon* (Row-Peterson), in 1912.

In 1908–1909, Gudrun Thorne-Thomsen was on leave from the University of Chicago to serve as a storyteller in branch libraries opened by the Chicago Public Library in park recreation buildings. These programs were jointly sponsored by the Chicago Public Library, the Chicago Association of Collegiate Alumnae, and the Chicago Woman's Club. The program was so successful that story hours became a regular part of the library's service to children. Her reputation as a gifted storyteller grew and Gudrun Thorne-Thomsen was invited to lecture on storytelling throughout the Midwest, California, Oregon, and Hawaii. She annually lectured on storytelling and folklore at the Western Reserve Library School and the Carnegie Library School of Pittsburgh. In 1923 she and her husband joined the faculty of the Ojai Valley School near Santa Barbara, California, and she became the school's first principal.

Soon after her husband's death in 1936, Gudrun Thorne-Thomsen retired as principal and launched a new career both as a visiting storyteller and as a recording artist for the Library of Congress and, later, for the Victor Company. Two books, *The Sky Bed* (Scribner) and *In Norway* (Viking), followed in the 1940s. In 1953 she was still training librarians in formal workshops and at informal gatherings in the art of storytelling.

"Perhaps the most wonderful thing of all," one of her students of that period reported, "was to make us feel that we could tell stories too; that it was not some difficult art to be mastered by only a few gifted individuals, but the rightful heritage of us all and a source of great joy."[14]

She died in 1956, but not before she knew—and took joy in the knowledge—that the Storytelling Festival to be held at Miami Beach during the 1956 American Library Association Conference planned to honor her with a day of storytelling. "You librarians who work with children," she wrote in acknowledgment of the honor, "I congratulate you on keeping alive the art of storytelling."[15]

Today, there are other notable storytellers, each of whom has a distinctive style, but love and respect for the art of storytelling are common to all.

Storytelling is still an integral part of the daily lives of people throughout the world. Stories are told in the marketplaces of Morocco, Nigeria, and India. In Japan the picture-showman calls the children with his wooden clapper and tells his stories with his picture cards. In Java the dalang still sings and chants the stories of the *Ramayana* as he works his puppets against a screen.

In the United States there has been a revival of the art of storytelling, a great oral tradition that needs neither gadgets, activities, nor the support of visual aids. Teachers and librarians, ever more aware of the relationship between hearing stories in childhood and a later love of reading, continue to tell stories to boys and girls in schools and libraries. Professional storytellers—that is, those who make their living solely or primarily through storytelling performance—travel across the country, telling stories in coffeehouses, concert halls, churches, museums, parks, and playgrounds, as well as in schools and libraries. Their performances are entertainment-oriented.

Annual storytelling events, such as the New York Public Library's storytelling symposium held early in May in honor of Marie Shedlock's birthday, the Storytelling Institute at the C. W. Post Center, Long Island University, the National Storytelling Festival held in Jonesborough, Tennessee, under the auspices of the National Association for the Preservation and Perpetuation of Storytelling (NAPPS), and A(ugusta) Baker's Dozen: A Celebration of Stories, sponsored by the Richland County Public Library, the College of Library and Information Science at the University of South Carolina, and the South Carolina State Library, have contributed to this revival. Storytelling schools, such as the Toronto School of Storytelling, the summer program of the National Association for the Preservation and Perpetuation of Storytelling, storytelling residencies, and courses in schools of librarianship and education offer opportunities for study of the art. The recently created National Clearinghouse for Information on Storytelling (NCIS) at East Carolina University will identify and organize information relevant to the storytelling community and make this information easily accessible to tellers and scholars. And folklorists interested in the collecting of oral history and stories, as well as in the performance aspect of storytelling, have provided a rich source of material for storytellers.

The art of storytelling, healthy and thriving today, was best described by Frances Clarke Sayers, who said, "It [storytelling] is a deathless art, lively and diverse, which like music, refreshes and revives those whom it touches even in its farthest reaches."[16]

## Notes

1. *The Panchatantra*, translated from the Sanskrit by Arthur Ryder (Chicago: University of Chicago Press, 1925), p. 16.
2. Anne Carroll Moore, *My Roads to Childhood: Views and Reviews of Children's Books* (New York: Doubleday, 1939), p. 145.
3. Ruth Hill, "Storytelling in the American Public Library" (manuscript in the files of the Office of Children's Services, New York Public Library).
4. Anne Carroll Moore, "Report on Storytelling," *Library Journal* 35 (September 1910): 408.
5. Ibid., p. 406.
6. Moore, *My Roads to Childhood*, p. 145.
7. Ibid.
8. Anna Cogswell Tyler, in a report dated 1909 in the files of the Office of Children's Services, New York Public Library.
9. Mary Rogers, in a letter in the files of the Office of Children's Services, New York Public Library.
10. Anne Carroll Moore, "Ruth Sawyer: Storyteller," *Horn Book Magazine*, January 1936, p. 37.
11. Virginia Haviland, *Ruth Sawyer* (New York: Walck, 1965), p. 22.
12. Moore, "Ruth Sawyer: Storyteller," p. 37.
13. Beryl Robinson, "Ruth Sawyer: 1880–1970," *Horn Book Magazine*, August 1970, p. 347.
14. Jasmine Britton, "Gudrun Thorne-Thomsen: Storyteller from Norway," *Horn Book Magazine*, February 1958, p. 27.

15. "Storytelling Festival at Miami Beach," *Top of the News*, October 1956, p. 17.

16. "Storytelling," in *Anthology of Children's Literature*, by Edna Johnson, Evelyn Sickels, and Frances Clarke Sayers (New York: Houghton, 1959), p. 1083.

## Titles Referred to in This Chapter

Bryant, Sara Cone. *How to Tell Stories to Children*. New York: Houghton, 1905; Detroit: Gale, 1973.

Davis, Mary Gould. *Truce of the Wolf*. New York: Harcourt, 1931, o.p.

Davis, Mary Gould, and Boggs, Ralph. *Three Golden Oranges and Other Spanish Folk Tales*. New York: Longmans, 1936, o.p.

Davis, Mary Gould, and Kalibala, Ernest. *Wakaima and the Clay Man*. New York: Longmans, 1946, o.p.

Sawyer, Ruth. *The Least One*. New York: Viking, 1941, o.p.

———. *The Long Christmas*. New York: Viking, 1941, o.p.

———. *My Spain: A Storyteller's Year of Collecting*. New York: Viking, 1967, o.p.

———. *Picture Tales from Spain*. New York: Viking, 1936, o.p.

———. *Roller Skates*. New York: Viking, 1936.

———. *Tonio Antonio*. New York: Viking, 1934, o.p.

———. *The Way of the Storyteller*. New York: Viking, 1942, 1962; rev. ed. Penguin, 1977.

Shedlock, Marie L. *The Art of the Story-Teller*. New York: Appleton, 1915; New York: Dover, 1951.

Thorne-Thomsen, Gudrun. *East of the Sun and West of the Moon*. Row-Peterson, 1912, o.p.

———. *In Norway*. New York: Viking, 1948, o.p.

———. *The Sky Bed*. New York: Scribner, 1944, o.p.

Tyler, Anna Cogswell. *Twenty-four Unusual Stories*. New York: Harcourt, 1921, o.p.

The authors wish to call to the reader's attention the May 1934 issue of *Horn Book Magazine* (volume 10, number 3), which was dedicated to Marie Shedlock.

# 2 Purpose and Values of Storytelling

Lewis Carroll called stories "love gifts." It was an apt description, for telling a story is, indeed, giving a gift. Storytelling brings to the listeners heightened awareness—a sense of wonder, of mystery, of reverence for life. This nurturing of the spirit-self comes first. It is the primary purpose of storytelling, and all other uses and effects are secondary.

Storytelling is a sharing experience. When we tell, we show our willingness to be vulnerable, to expose our deepest feelings, our values. That kind of nakedness that says you care about what you're relating invites children to listen with open minds and hearts. Enjoying a story together creates a common experience. Storytelling, properly done, produces a relaxed, restful feeling. It establishes a happy relationship between teller and listener, drawing people closer to one another, adult to child, child to child. This rapport carries over into other areas as well, for children tend to have confidence in the person who tells stories well.

From the very beginnings of library service to children, librarians recognized the possibilities in storytelling for introducing literature:

> Story-telling provides the opportunity to interpret for the child life forces which are beyond his immediate experience, and so to prepare him for life itself. It gives the teller the chance to emphasize significance rather than incident. It enables her, through the magic quality of the spoken word, to reveal to the child the charm and subtle connotations of word sounds, all the evanescent beauty emanating from combinations of words and from the cadence, the haunting ebb and flow, of rhythmical prose. It is through the medium of interpretation that all of us, adults and children, come to genuine appreciation. We approach the great, the significant, the infinite, through some mind more perceptive, more articulate than our own. That is the function of all art. It goes beyond the truth of fact to an all-embracing, unchanging truth, and it clothes this in a

beauty which heightens its poignancy, and which gains new beauty with the praise of each succeeding age. Story-telling, rightly done, is such an art.[1]

The storyteller works with words. The sound of words, the way an author puts words together to form a rhythmic pattern, please the ear and evoke a physical response from the young child. Research indicates that there is a connection between the development of motor ability and language competence. That there is such a relationship comes as no surprise to anyone who has ever held an infant and shared aloud Mother Goose rhymes. The young child responds to the rollicking verses with rhythmic movements of the body.

> To market, to market, to buy a fat pig,
> Home again, home again, jiggety-jig;
> To market, to market, to buy a fat hog,
> Home again, home again, jiggety-jog.

The enjoyment of sound and rhythm is enhanced by the sensuous pleasure of close body contact.

But Mother Goose rhymes have more to offer than rhythm and repetition. A Mother Goose rhyme is a minidrama. Consider, for example, "The Old Woman and Her Pig." This simple tale has characters, conflict, and action that lead to a climax and satisfying resolution. The old woman must persuade her obstinate pig to go over the stile so that she can get home. She appeals to quite ordinary objects—a stick, fire, water, rope—and to common animals—a dog, ox, rat, cat—for help. These usually inanimate objects and dumb animals act with a will of their own, entering into the conflict. The conflict is resolved when the old woman fills the cat's request for a saucer of milk, thus starting a sequence of events that culminates in the pig's jumping over the stile.

Children find pleasure in the way an author uses words to create mood, to evoke response, to create images that please the inward eye, as in the following three excerpts:

Whenever fairies are sad they wear white. And this year, which was long ago, was the year men were tearing down all the old zigzag rail fences. Now those old zigzag fences were beautiful for the fairies because a hundred fairies could sit on one rail and thousands and thousands of them could sit on the zigzags and sing pla-sizzy pla-sizzy, softer than an eye wink, softer than a baby's thumb, all on a moonlight summer night. And they found out that year was going to be the last year of the zigzag rail fences. It made them sorry and sad, and when they are sorry and sad they wear white. So they picked the wonderful white morning glories running along the zigzag rail fences and made them into little wristlets and wore those wristlets the next year to show they were sorry and sad.

From "How to Tell Corn Fairies When You See 'Em,"
in Carl Sandburg's *Rootabaga Stories*.[2]

Long, long ago the wind and the water were the closest of friends. Every day Mrs. Wind would visit Mrs. Water, and they would spend the day talking. Mostly they enjoyed talking about their children. Especially Mrs. Wind. "Just look at my children," Mrs. Wind would say. "I have big children and little children. They can go anywhere in the world. They can stroke the grass softly, and they can knock down a tree. They can go fast or they can go slowly. Nobody has children like mine."

From "Why the Waves Have Whitecaps," in
Julius Lester's *The Knee-High Man and Other Tales*.[3]

But that wasn't the end of Elsie Piddock; she has never stopped skipping on Caburn since, for Signed and Sealed is Signed and Sealed. Not many have seen her, because she knows all the tricks; but if you go to Caburn at the new moon, you may catch a glimpse of a tiny bent figure, no bigger than a child, skipping all by itself in its sleep, and hear a gay little voice, like the voice of a dancing yellow leaf, singing:

"Andy
Spandy
Sugardy
Candy
French
Almond
*Rock!*
Breadandbutterforyoursupper'sallyourmother'sGOT!"

From "Elsie Piddock Skips in Her Sleep," in Eleanor
Farjeon's *Martin Pippin in the Daisy Field*.[4]

The librarian or teacher storyteller has the pleasant responsibility of leading children to books. By making the connection between books and storytelling—by telling a story from a collection and saying more stories can be found in the book—the storyteller introduces books as a source of pleasure throughout life.

With so many children's books in print, it is possible for a child to read a great number without reading even one worthwhile book. Through storytelling we can introduce books of quality that otherwise might be missed. Storytelling can also benefit children who are ready for the literary experience a book offers before they are able to read it on their own. *Charlotte's Web* (Harper) is the classic example of a book that can be enjoyed on several levels. By the same token, children who are reluctant readers, who may never read either fiction or fantasy, have a share in literature through the experience of hearing stories told and read aloud.

Storytelling encourages the art of listening. Children experience the whole of a piece of literature, uninterrupted by questions or discussion. If the stories they hear are worth listening to, they are eager to learn the key that unlocks the symbols.

Studies of children who read early indicate that hearing stories told or read aloud in early childhood is a common factor. Listening to story books read aloud helps children to associate the symbols on the printed page with the words they are hearing. They also learn to follow events in sequence, and that print, in our society, reads from left to right.

Story listening may have an even greater significance in the young child's life. Howard Gardner writes in *The Arts and Human Development* (Wiley):

> . . . story hearing and telling is a very special, almost religious experience for the young child, one which commands his absolute attention and seems crucial in his mastery of language and his comprehension of the world. The child identifies fully with the characters and episodes in the stories and integrates them with situations encountered in the remainder of his working day, even as he incorporates names, events, rhythms, melodies, sounds, even entire passages into his night-time monologues. The central role played by story hearing and storytelling in the lives of most young children leads me to speculate that the narrative impulse plays an important role in organizing the child's world; and the auditory and vocalizing systems may require a certain amount of stimulation

which, though available from many sources, seems particularly
well satisfied by literary experience.[5]

Listening to stories introduces children to patterns of language and extends vocabulary. A kindergarten teacher who was
telling "One-Eye, Two-Eyes and Three-Eyes" to her class for a
second time said the mother was very "angry." The children cor-
rected her: "She was FURIOUS." The way the children pronounced
"furious" made it clear that their first meeting with the word was
in the story and that it made a strong impression on them.

A research project at New York University determined that
children speaking nonstandard English, especially those in kindergarten, expand their language ability dramatically when they
are involved in oral activities based on children's literature, such
as acting out a story, discussing its action, or performing in a puppet show. In another project students at Bank Street College of
Education found that story-reading experiences with children in a
child-care center where the children came from broken homes
built a positive attitude toward books and recognition of the pleasure that can be derived from them.

Hearing stories told gives children practice in visualization.
As children listen they create the scenes, the action, the characters. The ability to visualize, to fantasize, is the basis of creative
imagination. It also appears to have a positive effect on social and
cognitive development. Children with a strong predisposition toward imaginative play seem to empathize with other children
more readily. This is of special significance to educators who fear
that cognitive skills may have been emphasized in the past at the
expense of affective development. The noted Russian author and
specialist in children's language and literature, Kornei Chukovsky, believed the goal of storytelling to be "fostering in the
child, at whatever cost, compassion and humaneness—this mirac-
ulous ability of man to be disturbed by another being's misfor-
tunes, to feel joy about another being's happiness, to experience
another's fate as one's own."[6] (Figure 2.)

Storytelling gives children insight into the motives and patterns of human behavior. Bruno Bettelheim, in his book *The Uses
of Enchantment: The Meaning and Importance of Fairy Tales*, discusses

FIGURE 2. When children are enjoying a story their faces express interest, curiosity, delight. Story hour at a branch of the New York Public
Library. (Photograph © Bob Serating.)

the role of fairy tales in helping children master the psychological problems of growing up:

> A child needs to understand what is going on within his conscious self so that he can also cope with that which goes on in his unconscious. He can achieve this understanding, and with it the ability to cope, not through rational comprehension of the nature and content of his unconscious, but by becoming familiar with it through spinning out daydreams—ruminating, rearranging, and fantasizing about suitable story elements in response to unconscious pressures. By doing this, the child fits unconscious content into conscious fantasies, which then enable him to deal with that content. It is here that fairy tales have unequaled value, because they offer new dimensions to the child's imagination which would be impossible for him to discover as truly on his own. Even more important, the form and structure of fairy tales suggest images to the child by which he can structure his daydreams and with them give better direction to his life.[7]

Storytelling can lend support to the curriculum. However, this should be done in a natural way. Elizabeth Cook, in her book *The Ordinary and the Fabulous*, warns:

> It spoils the story of Odysseus to make it an introduction to a study of "real" eighth-century armour. The one natural point of contact is the historical date of writer or listener. There is nothing wrong in saying "And just at the time we were learning about, Homer told the story of Odysseus . . . and I'm going to read it to you now. . . ." Even so, it is better not to read too many legends of the same kind consecutively: children under eleven listen to them in the right spirit more easily if they are not assembled historically, but scattered over the syllabus and mixed up like poems in an anthology.[8]

Storytelling is a way of keeping alive the cultural heritage of a people. It is akin to the folk dance and the folk song in preserving the traditions of a country for the foreign-born child and of building appreciation of another culture for the native-born child. For instance, children who hear the story of *Perez and Martina* (Warne) are learning respect for Puerto Rican culture. Ann Nolan Clark, in her book *Journey to the People*, wrote:

Children need to know of other nationalities and races so that, inheriting an adult world, they find a free and joyous interchange of acceptance and respect among all peoples. . . . There is need for awareness that each group of people has its own special traditions and customs. There is need that respectful recognition be given these special traditions and customs. There is need for acceptance of these differences. There is tragic need for loving communion between children and children, children and adults, adults and adults—between group and group.[9]

Folklore is living proof of the kinship of human beings and the oneness of peoples. Among various nations, similar stories are found, but they assume a variety of forms according to the culture in which they have developed. Paul Bunyan is related to Ti-Jean. Over 300 years ago the French colonists brought the Ti-Jean stories to America; they soon became French-Canadian tales, and now they are part of the spoken tradition of the country. Glooscap was the hero-trickster of a great mythology shared by the Indians of Canada and the Indians in Maine and Massachusetts. And these stories show a likeness to both Norse and European folktales.

These are only a few of the many educational and psychological reasons for telling stories. The best reason of all, however, is the dramatic joy we bring to children and to ourselves. Good storytelling is, to the teller and listener alike, "to know joy unrestrained."[10]

## Notes

1. Elizabeth Nesbitt, "Hold to That Which Is Good," *Horn Book Magazine*, January–February 1940, p. 14.
2. Carl Sandburg, "How to Tell Corn Fairies When You See 'Em," in Sandburg, *Rootabaga Stories* (New York: Harcourt, 1951), p. 210.
3. Julius Lester, "Why the Waves Have Whitecaps," in Lester, *The Knee-High Man and Other Tales* (New York: Dial, 1972), p. 21.
4. Eleanor Farjeon, "Elsie Piddock Skips in Her Sleep," in Farjeon, *Martin Pippin in the Daisy Field* (Philadelphia: Lippincott, 1937), p. 81.
5. Howard Gardner, *The Arts and Human Development* (New York: Wiley, 1973), p. 203.
6. Kornei Chukovsky, *From Two to Five*, trans. and ed. by Miriam Morton (Berkeley: University of California Press, 1963), p. 138.
7. Bruno Bettelheim, *The Uses of Enchantment: The Meaning and Importance of Fairy Tales* (New York: Knopf, 1976), p. 7.

8. Elizabeth Cook, *The Ordinary and the Fabulous: An Introduction to Myths, Legends and Fairy Tales for Teachers and Storytellers*, 2nd ed. (New York: Cambridge University Press, 1976), p. 55.
9. Ann Nolan Clark, *Journey to the People* (New York: Viking, 1969), pp. 89, 27.
10. Ruth Sawyer, *The Way of the Storyteller* (New York: Viking, 1942), p. 148.

## Titles Referred to in This Chapter

Belpré, Pura. *Perez and Martina*. New York: Warne, 1961, o.p.
White, E. B. *Charlotte's Web*. New York: Harper, 1952.

# 3 Selection

Out of a rich reading background to select the story that exactly fits the day or the hour or the mood . . . that is to be a happy and successful storyteller. The ability to make the Story Hour a natural part of the life of a children's room, the experience that tells us how to group the children, how to protect them and ourselves from interruption, how to make the book that we tell the story from theirs as well as ours, how to recognize and direct the enthusiasm, the imagination and the faith that the story kindles—all these things become second nature after awhile. But the power to choose—that is very much harder to come by!

—*Mary Gould Davis*[1]

The power to choose involves knowledge of self, knowledge of storytelling literature, and knowledge of the group to whom one is telling.

Storytelling flows from a deep desire to share, the desire to be open about something that has touched one deeply. The choice of story and the manner in which it is told reveal one's inner self. Although the storyteller may be recreating a traditional tale, it is his or her experience of life that enters the telling and makes the story ring true. A soft-spoken, gentle young student chose to tell for her first story Grimm's "Fisherman and His Wife." Although she knew the plot perfectly she was unable to hold the children's attention, because she could not bring to her telling any understanding of the emotional makeup of the greedy wife. She made the wife's requests sound so reasonable that the dramatic conflict was lost and the children were bored. Sometime later in the course she told, successfully, Andersen's "Swineherd," a tale technically more difficult to learn and to tell. She was successful, because her empathy with the emotions dealt with in the story gave color to her telling.

The storyteller must take the story from the printed page and blow the breath of life into it. This cannot be done unless the story has meaning for the one who is telling it, because children are quick to sense one's true feelings about a story. The storyteller, then, must enjoy the content, mood, or style and must have a desire to share this enjoyment. Frances Clarke Sayers, who recalls listening to the story of "The Gingerbread Boy" as a child, remarks of the storyteller, "She told it as though she were relating a tale as great in magnitude as 'Hamlet,' as indeed it was for me, because it was for her. It was mystery, and tragedy, and delight."[2]

This knowing whether or not a story is right for you and your listeners is attained through trial and error—through the experience of telling and listening. But it also implies an enjoyment of storytelling literature and a wide knowledge of its background. A folktale is more likely to feel "right" if the storyteller has a thorough knowledge of the literature and the characteristics, customs, and ideals of the people or country from which the story has come. A literary fairy tale, on the other hand, requires that the storyteller empathize with the author. It is this genuine appreciation on the part of the storyteller that brings an intangible, personal quality to the telling of the story.

Finding stories one likes to tell may take more time than learning them. The storyteller reads constantly in search of new material. Rereading is important, too, because a story that may not appeal to the storyteller at first reading may appeal at another time.

There is a wide variety of literature to choose from: the great body of traditional literature—folktales, myths and legends, hero tales, fables, and drolls—and modern literature, such as the literary fairy tale, fantasy, fiction, and nonfiction, including biography. A long story can be broken down and told serially, or a single incident from a book may be selected for telling.

Poetry can be woven into the fabric of the story hour, offering fresh insights on the central theme, sharpening the senses—or it can stand on its own. It is made to be shared and not taught. The blending of poetry and folktales or fairy tales is a natural marriage, for both develop a child's imagination. Their combination in a single story hour can change the pace, create a mood, or add variety to the program. However, include a poem only if you truly like it, for false interest, dislike, and discomfort are all readily apparent to children.

Subject matter and concept must be considered in choosing poems, for these are the qualities that can place a poem beyond the comprehension and understanding of a child. On the other hand, many poems written for adults are appropriate to use in story hours for older boys and girls. As in the selection of stories, one must read widely in the area of poetry in order to make wise and appropriate selections.

There are poetry collections and poems for all ages, from Mother Goose to the Robin Hood ballads, from which to make a choice. Poems that have story content, strong rhythm, and descriptive language lend themselves well to the story hour. Quiet, gentle poems can set the mood for a special program. A nonsense poem sets the stage for a humorous story. Haiku is especially appropriate to the story hour, and its 17-syllable verse is often just right for a break between stories.

## What Makes a Story Tellable?

A good story for telling is one that has something to say and that says it in the best possible way. It is a story that has vision as well as integrity and that gives a child something to hold. There should be sound values—compassion, humor, love of beauty, resourcefulness, kindliness, courage, kinship with nature, zest for living—but they should be implicit in the story, because a good one is not didactic.

Some of the characteristics of a good story are:

1. A single theme, clearly defined.
2. A well-developed plot.

   A brief opening introduces the main characters, sets the scene, arouses pleasurable anticipation, and then, almost immediately, the story plunges into action.

   Action unfolds through word pictures, maintains suspense, and quickly builds to a climax. Each incident must be related in such a way that it makes a vivid and clear-cut image in the listener's mind. One event must lead logically and without interruption to the next. There should be no explanations or descriptions except where it is necessary for clearness. Avoid stories with flashbacks, subplots, or long descriptive passages that interfere with the flow of the story. The essential movement of the story must depend on events, not on attitudes.

The ending resolves the conflict, releases the tension, and leaves the listener feeling satisfied.

3. Style.

Look for vivid word pictures, pleasing sounds, rhythm.

4. Characterization.

The characters are believable, or, in the case of traditional folktales, they represent qualities, such as goodness, evil, beauty.

5. Faithfulness to source material.

Beware of the emaciated adaptation and the vocabulary-controlled tale.

6. Dramatic appeal.

Children need and enjoy a perfectly safe edge of fear and sadness. Marie Shedlock called storytelling "drama in miniature." She believed in satisfying the dramatic instincts of the child so that no child need say, as did one little girl, "It was no good; no one was killed. There were no lions, no tigers, no nothing at all."

7. Appropriateness for the listener.

A story's appeal depends on a child's age and interests. Restlessness often results from a poor choice. This criterion is developed at greater length in the pages that follow.

The youngest listeners, children from birth to age 3, enjoy stories with interesting sound patterns, such as *Good Night Moon*, by Margaret Wise Brown (Harper), and books that invite participation, such as *But Where Is the Green Parrot?*, by Thomas Zacharias and Wanda Zacharias (Delacorte). They like Mother Goose rhymes, simple folk songs, lullabies, and lilting poetry. Children from 3 to 5 years old respond to rhythm and repetition, simple direct plots in which familiarity is mixed with surprise, short dialogue, clear and simple images, action that quickly builds to a climax, and a satisfying ending. Young children blend fantasy with reality. In such a story as "The Three Bears," for instance, the chair and the bowl of porridge are familiar to children. Having them belong to the bears adds mystery and adventure to the story, but the situation is simple, and there are enough everyday events in it so that the children are not confused. They accept the unreal because it is close enough to the real world they know. The rhythm in stories for young children comes primarily from the repetition of words and phrases in a set pattern. Such phrases as, "Not by the hair of my chinny-chin-chin," "Then I'll huff and I'll puff and I'll blow your house in," and similar repetition in "The Three Billy Goats Gruff," "The Gingerbread Man," and "The Old Woman and Her Pig" emit a delighted response. Young children also enjoy stories like "The Bed," in which the sounds of animals are introduced.

The 6-, 7-, and 8-year-olds have a peak interest in traditional folktales and fairy tales, such as "One-Eye, Two-Eyes and Three-Eyes," "Cinderella," and "Mother Holle." F. André Favat found a close correspondence between the child's psychological characteristics at this stage in development and the characteristics of the folktale (i.e., egocentrism, and a belief in magic, animism, and retributive justice).[3] Through the story content they work through their inner fantasies and come to terms with the "real" world. Listening to these tales, they *are* Jack the Giant Killer or Molly Whuppie. The art form of the folktale also is very satisfying. In his introduction to *The Complete Grimm's Fairy Tales*, Padraic Colum discusses the patterns and rhymes in the folktales that make them so memorable. In "Rapunzel," for example, "the maiden has long hair and the witch confines her in a tower, and we do not know whether the tower makes it proper she should have long hair, or whether her long hair makes the tower part of the story." Good storytellers make the patterns evident. Mediocre storytellers "confuse the pattern by putting incidents in the wrong place, by using unfitting metaphors, by making a hurried beginning or a hurried end, by being unable to use the chiming words that made special, or, as we would say now, that featured some passage: 'puddle' with 'path,' 'tooth' with 'lose,' for example."[4]

The 9-to-11-year-olds enjoy the more sophisticated folktales, such as "Clever Manka," "Wicked John and the Devil," "Two of Everything," and many of the African folktales. The subtlety of African tales such as "The Woodcutter of Gura" is lost on children in the younger age groups, but they are excellent choices for young adult and adult audiences. It is important to be aware of dialogue and description when selecting the stories, because these two qualities identify the stories as being African. The trickster hare of Zaire and the spider trickster Anansi of Ghana both show that the weak can prevail over the strong. Stories about forces of nature appear in the Yoruba, the Ashanti, the Bantu, and other African cultures. An excellent source book is the adult title *A Treasury of African Folklore*, by Harold Courlander.[5] Its sub-title describes the range of material that is included in this book: "the oral literature—myths, legends, epics, tales, recollections, wisdom, sayings, and humor of Africa." It is a "must" for the storyteller's shelf. Here can be found the forerunners of the West Indian Anansi tales and the American Brer Rabbit.

The West Indian tales are a mixture of African, Carib and Arawak Indian, and European. These stories are lively, dramatic, witty, and humorous. Philip Sherlock, collector and author-editor of three collections, has provided an interesting introduction to these stories, in which the local pattern of speech has been modified without losing the rhythm and color of the islands. The Brer Rabbit stories, as told by Joel Chandler Harris, suffer from almost unintelligible author-created dialect, while "Mr. Rabbit and Mr. Bear" from Julius Lester's *The Knee-High Man* (Dial) and his *The Tales of Uncle Remus* (Dial), William J. Faulkner's *The Days When the Animals Talked* (Follett), and *The People Could Fly*, by Virginia Hamilton (Knopf), are good examples of tellable tales from the rich tradition of American black folk literature. *Bo Rabbit Smart for True* (Philomel) is retold by Priscilla Jaquith in the poetic, lilting language of Gullah.

Children over 9 are looking for something that will appeal to their developing power of reason and judgment and to their concern about competency. These children enjoy the hero tales, myths, and legends. This is the time to introduce the retellings of the *Odyssey* by Padraic Colum and the legends of Robin Hood and King Arthur, as retold by Howard Pyle. The exaggerated humor of the tall tale is appreciated. Stories about Davy Crockett, Paul Bunyan, Pecos Bill, and John Henry should be told as if they were the "gospel truth."

Slightly older children, the 11-to-13-year-olds, are experiencing sexual awakening and are involved in a search for personal identity. The romantic stories of Eleanor Farjeon, the bittersweet fairy tales of Laurence Housman, the more elaborate tales from the *Arabian Nights*, the modern fairy tales of Jane Yolen, and the sly humor of Natalie Babbitt's stories about the Devil are enjoyed by these young people, who are ready to appreciate the development of the plot, the beauty of language, and the deeper meanings that lie behind the words.

## What Kinds of Stories Are Needed in a Storyteller's Repertoire?

A storyteller must be flexible, as it is often necessary to change a program at the last minute. The makeup of the group may not be what the storyteller expected, or the time allotted for the program may have to be shortened or expanded. In building a repertoire, new tellers will want to include various types of stories: action stories, romances, hero tales, "why" or *pourquoi* stories, humorous stories, short "encore" stories, and stories that appeal to a wide age range.

Though storytellers will need to have different types of stories in their repertoires for different occasions, they often find that they feel more comfortable with certain kinds of stories than with others. Stories from one's own national or regional background are usually a happy choice.

The beginning storyteller would do well to turn to folktales, stories that have been passed down through word of mouth and polished over centuries of telling. These traditional tales have the essentials of a good short story: terseness, simplicity, and vigor. They begin simply, come to the point, and end swiftly and conclusively. They are full of action, and the action is carried forward by the main characters. There are no unnecessary words, but only the right ones, to convey the beauty, the mood, the atmosphere of the tale.

These stories come from the folk—workers, peasants, just plain people. They are as old as the human race. Though they were told primarily to amuse, they also contain the key to the ideas, customs, and beliefs of earlier peoples, for life then was told in a tale, not explained in a philosophy. Thus the folktale is enhanced by simplicity and directness—and this is the way it should be.

The qualities and atmosphere of the country in which they originate and the differences that natural environment and racial character make in the development of imaginative literature can be seen in a comparison of the following two excerpts from folk-tales:

> Across the wide sea-ocean, on the further side of high mountains, beyond thick forests, in a village that faced the sky, there once lived an old peasant who had three sons.
>
> From "The Little Humpbacked Horse,"
> in Post Wheeler's *Russian Wonder Tales.*[6]

At once we are in Russia, that land of vast distances. What a different mood this scene evokes:

> Ol-Ambu followed a path that led to the grassland. Where the forest ended and the plains spread out before him, he stopped. He looked over the sea of brown grass with acacia trees and thorn-bushes scattered over it. And his eyes fell upon the largest giraffe he had ever seen.
>
> From "Ol-Ambu and He-of-the-Long-
> Sleeping-Place," in Verna Aardema's *Tales for the Third Ear: From Equatorial Africa.*[7]

Likewise, the storyteller can convey to children the kinship of peoples by telling variants of well-loved tales, such as "Cinderella" ("Ashputtel," "Vasilisa the Beautiful," "Nomi and the Magic Fish") and "Rumpelstiltskin" ("Tom Tit Tot," "Whipperty Stourie," "The White Hen").

The storyteller of some experience, or the beginning storyteller who has an affinity for certain authors, will also tell literary fairy tales.

The literary fairy tale is a consciously created work of art by a known author. It bears the stamp of individuality that immediately sets it apart from others. Hans Christian Andersen, Eleanor Farjeon, Laurence Housman, Carl Sandburg, Oscar Wilde, and contemporary writers Natalie Babbitt, Isaac Bashevis Singer, Barbara Picard, and Jane Yolen are among those who have distinguished themselves in this genre.

The modern fairy tale does not invariably end happily; often it leaves one thoughtful and sad. Told sensitively, reflecting the writer's own attitudes, many of the literary stories are vivid, accurate commentaries on society and the individuals who struggle within it. Characters in these modern imaginative stories are individuals with distinct personalities, as opposed to the stock characters we meet in the folktale.

Literary fairy tales tend to be longer and more descriptive than folktales. The words are filled with the beauty of sound, for the writer of the literary fairy tale is a word stylist. If the order of the words is altered, the beauty may be lost.

Some literary fairy tales are almost like folktales. Their writers base their style on folklore and do it so successfully that their stories may be as universal a choice as the folktales themselves. Howard Pyle was a writer who used the manner of the folktale. His collection *The Wonder Clock* (Harper) is built on what folklorists call the framing story. His preface begins, "I put on my dream-cap one day and stepped into Wonderland." The whole of this preface, with its power to set the stage and to convey atmosphere, should be told before each of the stories. Then let the old clock strike and tell the story that you have selected, letting the children feel that, beyond your selection, there are 23 other tales just as good or better.

Howard Pyle used the rhythm of folklore and its repetition. In "The Swan Maiden," the king's son mounts the wild swan and then:

> On flew the swan, and on and on, until, by and by, she said: "What do you see, king's son?"
>
> "I see the grey sky above me and the dark earth below me, but nothing else," said he.
>
> So once more they flew on until the Swan Maiden said, for the third time, "And what do you see by now, king's son?"
>
> By this time the prince said, "I see the grey sky above me and the dark earth below me, and over yonder is a glass hill, and on the hill is a house that shines like fire."
>
> "That is where the witch with the three eyes lives," said the Swan Maiden.
>
> From "The Swan Maiden," in Howard Pyle's *The Wonder Clock*.[8]

In *Tales Told Again* (Knopf), Walter de la Mare has taken 19 familiar folktales and touched them subtly with his genius. An English countryside seems the perfect setting for his humorous elaboration of the old fable in which the hedgehog beats the quick-footed but slow-witted hare; the hedgehog has his wife (who looks exactly like her husband) wait at one end of the field while he remains at the other. Every time the hare arrives at either end of the field, he sees the hedgehog, or so he thinks, and hears his laughing taunt, "Ahah! So here you are again! At last!" Errol Le Cain's handsome picture book edition of de la Mare's retelling of "Molly Whuppie" is a fine introduction to this writer for younger listeners.

## What Types of Stories Appeal to Groups in Which There Is a Wide Age Range?

Stories that can be enjoyed on different levels are good choices for the story-hour group composed of mixed ages. Younger children enjoy the plot and action, whereas older children enjoy the subtleties of humor and the interplay among characters. Younger children, hearing the story "Two of Everything" from *The Treasure of Li-Po*, by Alice Ritchie (Harcourt), marvel at the pot that can make two of anything the old couple put into it, whereas older children—and adults—are amused by the couple's plight when another wife steps out of the pot! In Harold Courlander's "Uncle Bouqui Rents a Horse," young children find the mental image of two large families plus livestock loaded down on the horse great fun. Older children appreciate the outwitting of Uncle Bouqui. In presenting these stories, the storyteller should emphasize the aspects of the story that will appeal most to a particular group of listeners.

## Where Can a Storyteller Find Stories That Have Known Appeal to Children?

There are many lists of stories. Two of the most helpful to the neophyte are *Stories: A List of Stories to Tell and to Read Aloud* (New York Public Library) and *Stories to Tell to Children: A Selected List* (Carnegie Library of Pittsburgh).

*Stories* is an annotated list, arranged alphabetically by story title. The annotations evoke the flavor of the stories. The list also includes bibliographies of background reading for the storyteller, poetry and stories for reading aloud, and recordings of stories. It is indexed by types of stories, such as "Clever and Heroic

Women," "Action and Participation Stories," "Christmas," and others.

*Stories to Tell to Children* is arranged by age level and by types of stories. Suitability of material for radio and television is noted. Variants of the tales are given for many of the entries. No annotations are given.

Each of these lists is based on a program of regular story hours held over a period of more than 75 years. They represent the children's choices. Storytellers will want to have copies of both lists on their personal book shelves. Collections compiled by storytellers with extensive experience are also an excellent source for beginning storytellers (see Appendix 2).

## How Does a Storyteller Develop Critical Ability?

The storyteller is someone who appreciates literature as a whole and knows good language, form, and substance. Critical ability is developed by reading widely and by constantly comparing recommended versions included on storytelling lists with newly published material. Careful attention should be given to the notes in collections by reputable compilers, such as Joseph Jacobs, Harold Courlander, and Richard Chase, and by reputable translators, such as Erik Haugaard and Elizabeth Shub.

Critical listening is developed by reading aloud various versions of the same story and selecting the one that sounds best. Listening to recordings made by fine storytellers gives one a sense of good pacing and the importance of word tone.

## How Does a Storyteller Recognize the Best Version or Translation of a Story?

Every year dozens of new translations or new retellings of the old tales come into our hands. We need to test them first in the light of our own personal knowledge of folk literature, then by their vitality and their holding power with children. This knowledge is based on continual study and reading of storytelling literature.

The folktales we share with children are polished retellings of "raw" folklore. However, the versions we choose must catch the flavor of the people from which the tales come and must give a feeling for what those people value. The language should flow in the cadence of the original tongue. Look for collections in which the compiler gives the sources of the stories and adds explanatory notes about the background of the tales. Brian Alderson's meticulous editing of Andrew Lang's color fairy books is a touchstone.

In selecting epics or hero tales, storytellers must be thoroughly familiar with different versions. Often they will have to make their own arrangement of the material, weaving together episodes from the various stories told about the hero, whether he be Robin Hood, King Arthur, or Cuchulain, that have come down by way of tradition.

Myths should reflect the people from which they originated. Compare Penelope Proddow's translation of *Demeter and Persephone* (Doubleday) with Nathaniel Hawthorne's version in his *Tanglewood Tales* (Dutton). Hawthorne embroiders the tale and diminishes the gods. Proddow retains the story's classic beauty.

Language should be beautiful, colorful, and descriptive. Compare the following two versions of "The Golden Goose":

> There was once a man who had three sons, the youngest of whom was called the Simpleton. He was laughed at and despised and neglected on all occasions. Now it happened one day that the eldest son wanted to go into the forest, to hew wood, and his Mother gave him a beautiful cake and a bottle of wine to take with him, so that he might not suffer from hunger or thirst. When he came to the wood he met a little old grey man, who, bidding him good-day, said: "Give me a small piece of the cake in your wallet, and let me drink a mouthful of your wine; I am so hungry and thirsty." But the clever son answered: "If I were to give you my cake and my wine, I should have none for myself, so be off with you," and he left the little man standing there and walked away. Hardly had he begun to cut down a tree, when his axe slipped and cut his arm, so that he had to go home at once and have the wound bound up. This was the work of the little grey man.
>
> From L. Leslie Brooke's *The Golden Goose Book*.[9]

Now read the same part of the story from *Favorite Fairy Tales to Read Aloud* (Grosset):

> There was once a man who had three sons, the youngest of whom was called Dummling.

One day, the eldest son decided to go into the forest to cut some wood. Before he started his mother packed a lunch for him so that he might not suffer from hunger or thirst.

In the wood at midday, he stopped work and sat down to eat. Just then, a little old man appeared before him and said, "May I have a crust of bread and some milk? I am so hungry and thirsty."

But the young man said, "If I do, I shan't have enough for myself. Be off with you!"

He left the little man standing there and went on his way. But he had not been long at work, chopping down a tree, before he cut himself and had to go home to have it bandaged.

Now this was no accident. It was brought about by the little man, who had magic powers, and had decided that anyone as selfish as this fellow should be punished.

> From "The Golden Goose," in *Favorite Fairy Tales to Read Aloud.*[10]

The second version has had a stamp of approval put upon it by a "distinguished panel" of experts that includes two educators and one librarian. But how much of the color and beauty of style will be lost to the child who hears this version rather than the other!

Another pitfall to avoid is the vocabulary-controlled book. Compare the following two versions of Hans Christian Andersen's "Ugly Duckling":

It was so beautiful out in the country. It was summer—the wheat fields were golden, the oats were green, and down among the green meadows the hay was stacked. There the stork minced about on his red legs, clacking away in Egyptian, which was the language his mother had taught him. Round about the field and meadow lands rose vast forests, in which deep lakes lay hidden. Yes, it was indeed lovely out there in the country.

In the midst of the sunshine there stood an old manor house that had a deep moat around it. From the walls of the manor right down to the water's edge great burdock leaves grew and there were some so tall that little children could stand upright beneath the biggest of them. In this wilderness of leaves, which was as dense as the forest itself, a duck sat on her nest, hatching her ducklings. She was becoming somewhat weary, because sitting is such dull business and scarcely anyone came to see her. The other ducks would much rather swim in the moat than waddle out and squat under a burdock leaf to gossip with her.

But at last the eggshells began to crack, one after another. "Peep, peep!" said the little things, as they came to life and poked out their heads.

"Quack, quack!" said the duck, and quick as quick can be they all waddled out to have a look at the green world under the leaves. Their mother let them look as much as they pleased, because green is good for the eyes.

From "The Ugly Duckling" in *The Complete Andersen: All of the 168 Stories by Hans Christian Andersen*, trans. by Jean Hersholt.[11]

The second version is from a Read-It-Myself book:

Once upon a time there was a mother duck. The mother duck had some eggs. "Quack, quack," said Mother Duck. "I must sit on my eggs. I must sit on my eggs a long time. One day the eggs will crack. Then little ducklings will jump out of the eggs."

So Mother Duck sat and sat. She sat on the eggs a long time. Then one egg began to crack. "Crack, crack" went the egg. "Crack, crack, crack." A little duckling jumped out.

"Jump, jump," went the duckling.

Mother Duck was so happy. "Quack, quack," said Mother Duck. "Quack, quack, quack." "Peep, peep," said the duckling. Soon another egg began to crack.

From Hans Christian Andersen's *The Ugly Duckling*, adapted by Frances K. Pavel.[12]

The story continues in this vein until all the eggs are hatched.

Yes, the child can easily read the second version, but as Clifton Fadiman has said, "What the child-mind measurers call a feeling of mastery is often only a feeling of boredom."[13] A simple but graceful retelling of Andersen's story for children to read on their own is *The Ugly Duckling*, retold by Lilian Moore (Scholastic).

The storyteller rejects the versions with undistinguished language and uses the ones with smooth, rhythmic style and language that add to the musical flow of the story.

### What Is Fractured Storytelling?

Fractured stories are modernized renditions of traditional tales. They are often witty or bizarre. The tale may be told from the viewpoint of another character in the story; for instance,

"Hansel and Gretel" might be told from the viewpoint of the witch. Or the tale might be placed in a modern setting with hip characters speaking the latest slang. Fractured tellings, such as those found in *Foxy Fables*, by Tony Ross (Dial), and *Roald Dahl's Revolting Rhymes* (Knopf), are fun to share with older listeners who are familiar with the traditional versions. Younger listeners need to hear the traditional versions. They are part of every child's literary heritage.

## Notes

1. Mary Gould Davis, "The Art of Storytelling" (paper delivered at a meeting of the American Library Association, Washington, D.C., May 15, 1929).
2. Frances Clarke Sayers, *Summoned by Books: Essays and Speeches* (New York: Viking, 1965), p. 96.
3. F. André Favat, *Child and Tale: The Origins of Interest* (Urbana, Ill.: National Council of Teachers of English, 1977).
4. Padraic Colum, "Introduction," in *The Complete Grimm's Fairy Tales* (New York: Pantheon, 1976), p. ix.
5. Harold Courlander, *A Treasury of African Folklore* (New York: Crown, 1975).
6. Post Wheeler, "The Little Humpbacked Horse," in Wheeler, *Russian Wonder Tales* (New York: Beechhurst, 1946), p. 67.
7. Verna Aardema, "Ol-Ambu and He-of-the-Long-Sleeping-Place" in Aardema, *Tales for the Third Ear: From Equatorial Africa* (New York: Dutton, 1969), pp. 59–60.
8. Howard Pyle, "The Swan Maiden," in Pyle, *The Wonder Clock* (New York: Harper, 1887, 1915), pp. 232–233.
9. L. Leslie Brooke, *The Golden Goose Book* (New York: Warne, 1905), unpaged.
10. "The Golden Goose," in *Favorite Fairy Tales to Read Aloud* (New York: Grosset, 1958), pp. 5–6.
11. Hans Christian Andersen, *The Complete Andersen: All of the 168 Stories by Hans Christian Andersen*, trans. by Jean Hersholt (New York: Heritage, 1942, 1949), pp. 177–178, pink section.
12. Hans Christian Andersen, *The Ugly Duckling*, adapted by Frances K. Pavel (New York: Holt, 1961), pp. 1–4.
13. Clifton Fadiman, "Holiday Handbook of Children's Reading," *Holiday* 30 (November 1961): 148.

## Titles Referred to in This Chapter

Andersen, Hans Christian. *The Ugly Duckling*. Retold by Lilian Moore. Illustrated by Daniel San Souci. New York: Scholastic, 1987.

Brown, Margaret Wise. *Good Night Moon*. Illustrated by Clement Hurd. New York: Harper, 1947.

Cathon, Laura, ed. *Stories to Tell to Children: A Selected List*, 8th ed. Pittsburgh: University of Pittsburgh Press for Carnegie Library of Pittsburgh, 1974.

Courlander, Harold. *A Treasury of African Folklore*. New York: Crown, 1975.

Dahl, Roald. *Roald Dahl's Revolting Rhymes*. Illustrated by Quentin Blake. New York: Knopf, 1983.

De la Mare, Walter. *Molly Whuppie*. Illustrated by Errol Le Cain. New York: Farrar, 1983.

———. *Tales Told Again*. New York: Knopf, 1959; Winchester, Mass.: Faber, 1980.

Faulkner, William J. *The Days When the Animals Talked: Black American Folktales and How They Came to Be*. New York: Follett, 1977.

Hamilton, Virginia. *The People Could Fly: American Black Folktales*. Illustrated by Leo Dillon and Diane Dillon. New York: Knopf, 1985.

Hawthorne, Nathaniel. *Tanglewood Tales*. New York: Dutton, 1950; London: Dent, 1974.

Iarusso, Marilyn. *Stories: A List of Stories to Tell and to Read Aloud*, 7th ed. New York: New York Public Library, 1977.

Jaquith, Priscilla. *Bo Rabbit Smart for True: Folktales from the Gullah*. New York: Philomel, 1981.

Lang, Andrew. *Blue Fairy Book*. Edited by Brian Alderson. New York: Viking, 1978.

———. *Green Fairy Book*. Edited by Brian Alderson. New York: Viking, 1978.

———. *Pink Fairy Book*. Edited by Brian Alderson. New York: Viking, 1982.

———. *Red Fairy Book*. Edited by Brian Alderson. New York: Viking, 1978.

———. *Yellow Fairy Book*. Edited by Brian Alderson. New York: Viking, 1980.

Lester, Julius. *The Knee-High Man and Other Tales*. New York: Dial, 1972.

———. *The Tales of Uncle Remus: The Adventures of Brer Rabbit*. New York: Dial, 1987.

MacManus, Seumas. *Hibernian Nights*. New York: Macmillan, 1963, o.p.

Proddow, Penelope. *Demeter and Persephone: Homeric Hymn Number Two*. New York: Doubleday, 1972, o.p.

Pyle, Howard. *The Wonder Clock*. New York: Harper, 1887; New York: Dover, 1965.

Ritchie, Alice. *The Treasure of Li-Po*. New York: Harcourt, 1949, o.p.

Ross, Tony. *Foxy Fables*. New York: Dial, 1986.

Zacharias, Thomas. *But Where Is the Green Parrot?* New York: Delacorte, 1978.

# 4 Preparation

Storytelling is an art and, like all arts, it requires training and experience. However, anyone who is willing to take the time to find the right story and learn it well, and who has a sincere desire to share enjoyment of the story, can be a successful storyteller. A good part of our daily conversation is composed of stories, incidents, and anecdotes, for we are all storytellers a few steps removed from professional storytellers. Our language is somewhat less formalized, but we are still sharing our experiences and emotions.

## The Basic Approaches to Learning a Story

Storytelling is an individual art. Storytellers develop different methods of learning stories. However, there seem to be two basic approaches: the visual and the auditory. In the visual approach, the storyteller sees the story in a series of pictures, much like the frames of a filmstrip. In learning the story of "The Woman Who Flummoxed the Fairies," for example, the storyteller might see the following pictures:

1. the woman baking cakes and pastries for a wedding or a christening
2. the fairies longing for a bit of her cake and plotting to steal her away to be their baker
3. the woman baking cakes in the castle kitchen for the great wedding
4. the fairies hiding in flower cups and under leaves along the woman's path home
5. the fairies flying out at the woman and drifting fern seed in her eyes to make her sleepy
6. the woman asleep on the fairy mound
7. the woman waking up in fairyland and pretending to be happy and willing to bake a cake for the fairies

8. the woman asking the fairies to fetch things from her kitchen so that she can bake a cake for them
9. the fairies fetching the eggs, sugar, flour, butter, bowl, wooden spoons, and egg whisk, till they are tired out.
10. the woman asking first for her cat, then for her dog, her babe, and finally her husband
11. the woman beating the cake batter, the baby screaming, the cat purring, the dog snoring, and the husband looking bewildered
12. complete bedlam—the woman giving the baby the spoon to bang with, the husband pinching the dog and treading on the tail of the cat
13. the fairies exhausted by the noise
14. the woman asking for an oven
15. the fairies letting her and her family go home after she promises to leave the cake by the fairy mound for the fairies
16. the woman and her family at home and content
17. the woman leaving the cake behind the fairy mound and finding the little brown bag of gold pieces the fairies left for her
18. the woman baking a cake every week for the fairies and receiving a bag of gold pieces in return
19. everyone living happily ever after.[1]

In the auditory approach, the storyteller is conscious of the sound of words and their arrangement. A break in the rhythm is a warning that the telling is off track. Those who use this approach often record the story on tape before learning it. Playing back the tape in relaxed moments or while doing undemanding chores facilitates the learning process. A word of caution may be in order for the neophyte. It is best to be sure that you want to be a storyteller *before* you tape. The tape will bring out every imperfection of voice and timing. Do not be discouraged. If the story you have chosen to learn has been recorded by a professional storyteller, you may prefer to listen to it until you have gained confidence in yourself. There are many outstanding recordings of stories available (see Appendix 2).

The beginning storyteller who has a great deal of self-confidence may wish to videotape the story. The videotape captures facial mannerisms and gestures as well as imperfections of voice and timing. It is a harsh learning tool but a very helpful one, provided you do not let it rob you of the pleasure of sharing the story. Videotaping is probably more helpful to the experienced storyteller who wants to perfect style and technique.

Perhaps this is an appropriate place to mention mechanical devices, other than tape recorders, that storytellers may find helpful. Some storytellers claim that typing a story makes a carbon copy of it on the mind. Others find that outlining the story impresses it on the mind and serves as a quick refresher of memory when the story is told at a later date. This may be a formal outline or a freely written-out version. A storyboard is also a good memory jogger (see Chapter 7).

Cue cards may be used. As you read, whenever you come across a story you enjoy and want to learn, make a 4-by-6-inch card with the following information: title, author, source, running time, characters, scenes, synopsis, and any rhymes or characteristic phrases you wish to memorize. (Figure 3.)

| | |
|---|---|
| Title: | "The Frog Prince" |
| Author: | Brothers Grimm |
| Source: | *Tales from Grimm*, trans. and illus. by Wanda Gág (Coward, 1936) |
| Running time: | 8 minutes (determined by reading the story aloud) |
| Characters: | Princess, Frog Prince, King |
| Scenes: | Well under the linden tree |
| | Dinner table at the palace—repeated |
| | Bedroom of the Princess—repeated |
| Synopsis: | When the Princess loses her golden ball in the well, the frog rescues it on condition that the Princess will allow him to eat from her golden plate and sleep in her own little bed. The Princess is forced to keep her promise. On the third morning the spell is broken, and the frog changes into a handsome young Prince. When the Princess and the Prince grow up, they marry and live happily ever after. |
| Rhymes: | "Youngest Daughter of the King |
| | Open the door for me |
| | Mind your words at the old well spring |
| | Open the door for me."[2] |
| Audience: 6–8-year-olds | |

FIGURE 3. Sample cue card.

Choreographing, that is, marking the story to indicate voice inflections, pace, and timing, is another technique. Storyteller Carol Birch comments, "When first learning a story, I am very formal about modulation. I search for the best way to create the effect I want. In this way I shape a story from the beginning, noting places to pause, lines that come quickly, words that need emphasis, places to raise or lower my voice. This is like a musician working with phrasing and tempos, for a story changes with each telling, as music changes with each performance." (See example from Laurence Housman's "The Wooing of the Maze,"[3] Figure 4.)

## Basic Steps in Learning a Story

Allow time each day over a period of at least two to three weeks to make a new story your own. Live with your story until the characters and the setting become as real to you as people and places you know. Know it so well that it can be told as if it were a personal reminiscence.

Read the story from beginning to end several times. Read it for pleasure first. Then read it over with concentration. Analyze the story to determine where the appeal lies, what the art form is, what word pictures you want your listeners to see, what mood you wish to create. Before learning a story, Gudrun Thorne-Thomsen would ask herself what it was about the story that she wanted to share with children. Was it humor, even nonsense? The sense of wonder? Beauty? What was its essential quality? Whatever the particular quality and appeal of the story, the storyteller must have responded to it, sensed it, felt it intimately before giving it out again.

Read the story aloud and time it. Time it again when you begin to tell it. Some variation in time of reading and telling is to be expected, but if the telling takes much less time than the reading, it may indicate that parts have been omitted or that you are speaking too quickly. If it takes much longer, you may have added to the tale or you are speaking too slowly.

Learn the story as a whole rather than in fragments. Master the structure of the story. Perceive the story line. The story line consists of the beginning, which sets the stage and introduces the characters and conflict; the body, in which the conflict builds up

That same day/the Princess, sitting upon her throne
and having crown and scepter in her hands, caused the
gardener to be called into her presence. The courtiers
thought it was very strange that the Princess should *GRAND*
have a thing of such importance to make known to a
gardener that it was necessary for her to receive him with *like sucking on a lemon* *naughty*
crown and throne and scepter, as if it were an affair of
state.

*gossipy quick*

To the gardener, when he stood before her, she said,
"Gardener, it is my wish that there should be fashioned *sly*
for me a very great maze, so intricate and deceitful that
no man who has not the secret of it shall be able to pene-
trate therein. Inmost is to be/a little tower/and foun- *softcn* *wistful see each detail*
tains/and borders of sweet-smelling flowers and herbs. *sweet*
But the man who fashions this maze and has its secret
must remain in it forever lest he should betray his knowl- *unsure halting*
edge to others. So it is my will that (you) should devise *breathless*
such a maze for my delight and be yourself the prisoner *hopeful*
of your own craft when it is accomplished.") *intense, she is prisoner to her heart – he has the key*

FIGURE 4. Choreographed portion of "The Wooing of the Maze," in *The
Rat-Catcher's Daughter: A Collection of Stories by Laurence Housman* (Atheneum), selected by Ellin Greene.

to the climax; and the resolution of the conflict. Do not alter the essential story line. Note how the action starts, how it accelerates, how and where the transitions occur. Note sequences of names and events. Know absolutely what the successive steps are in the course of action. Test yourself by closing the book and making a list of these steps in proper order.

Master the style of the story. To retain the original flavor and vigor, memorize rhymes of characteristic phrases that recur throughout the story, such as these two:

> Be bold, be bold, but not too bold,
> Lest that your heart's blood should run cold.
>> From "Mr. Fox," in Joseph Jacobs's *English Fairy Tales*.[4]

> Now with cold grows faint her breath,
> Fire will conquer frosted death.
>> From "The Magic Ball," in Charles J. Finger's *Tales from Silver Lands*.[5]

Observe the sentence structure, phrases, unusual words and expressions. The beginning and ending are important. You may want to memorize them. "Crick crack," says the storyteller on the Caribbean island of Martinique, and the children reply, "Break my back." "Once there was and twice there wasn't, when genies played polo in the old Turkish bath, when the camel was a salesman and the flea a barber . . ." is one traditional way of beginning a Turkish tale. "So of course they lived, as why should they not, happily ever after," and "He was then married to the king's daughter, and the wedding lasted nine days, nine hours, nine minutes, nine half minutes and nine quarter minutes, and they lived happy and well from that day to this," are characteristic endings.

Make the story your own. Become familiar with the characters and the scenes. Build in your imagination the setting of your story. What are the main characters like? Are they clever, kind, greedy, timid, mischievous? How are they dressed? How do they speak—in vernacular, short sentences, pompously? Visualize the happenings. Reproduce these happenings as though you were seeing and experiencing them. Imagine sounds, tastes, scents, colors. Only when you see the story vividly yourself can you make your audience see it. Eulalie Steinmetz Ross advised:

> Bring to the telling of the story any experience, any memory, any knowledge from life that will give breadth and depth to its interpretation. Hear the Sleeping Beauty Waltz as the French fairy tale weaves its spell of enchantment. See the Chicago skyline as the background for Carl Sandburg's "Two Skyscrapers Who Decided to Have a Child." Remember the lines of Robert Frost's poem, "Stopping by Woods . . ." as you tell Mary Wilkins' "The Silver Hen." Train yourself to see, and you unconsciously give your audience time to see also. The pace of the story will come to fit the action and the scene. You must give the story depth and conviction, setting and atmosphere, before you can make it live for your audience.[6]

Miming the actions, characters, and emotions develops a kinesthetic sense of the story that enhances the telling.

Timing is the dramatic part of storytelling. Each story has its own pace; for example, "Sleeping Beauty" is slow and stately, "The Gingerbread Man" is sprightly, "Robin Hood" is strong and firm. Good timing makes the difference between the neophyte and the accomplished storyteller. Herein lies the value of listening to recordings by notable storytellers.

A few suggestions about timing:

1. Pause before any change of idea, before any significant word.
2. Emphasize words that carry meaning.
3. In general, poetic and imaginative passages should be taken slowly; parts narrating action should be taken rapidly.
4. Build toward the climax. Change pace as you near it so that your listeners may know the pleasure of anticipation. Some climaxes are made more impressive by a gradual slowing down. Others are highlighted by speeding up the rate of telling. Knowing whether to slow down or speed up comes with experience and sensitivity.
5. Conversation should be taken at a speed that is appropriate for the character speaking. Beginning storytellers often are afraid of using pauses, but when they are handled well, pauses can add drama and meaning, and they do not suggest nervousness or hesitancy.

6. Remember that the pause and a dropped voice can be more effective than the shout.

Practice telling the story aloud—to yourself, your pet, your family and friends, to anyone who will listen! Any hesitation reveals weak areas in your knowledge of the story. Practice wherever and whenever you can—while waiting in the doctor's or dentist's office, while traveling on public transportation, while doing undemanding chores. Ignore the stares of strangers, friends, family! Practice, practice, practice. As a final aid, just before going to sleep at night, read the story as printed in the book, slowly and aloud.

Practice in front of a mirror to catch distracting mannerisms. Gestures should be natural to the story and to the storyteller. The art of storytelling should not be confused with the art of acting. The storyteller interprets and expresses the ideas, moods, and emotions of the author, but never identifies with any character. The storyteller is not an actor or actress but the medium through which the story is passed. There should be no studied gestures, no gimmicks, no tricks of changing voices to suit each character in the story. These only tend to distract from the story. Storytelling is a folk art and does not lend itself to the grand gestures of the stage. Mary Gould Davis used to say to her students, "There are no Broadway talent scouts sitting in the audience of children."

Tone of voice should relate to what is going on in the story. The storyteller develops a sensitivity to words. Feel the appropriate emotion when you sound words so that the word "dull," for example, has a dullness about it. Train your ear to hear rhythmic phrases. The skipping-rope rhyme in "Elsie Piddock Skips in Her Sleep" should be chanted in time to a jump rope.

How you use your breath is important. Place your voice somewhere near the middle of the chest rather than in the head or upper chest. Breathing from the upper chest or head will give you a lighter, weaker tone; breathing from the abdomen will give you rich, full tones, connoting strength and vigor. Instead of assuming different voices for different characters, suggest characters by the amount of breath used. For example, instead of using a high-pitched squeaky voice for the wee little bear in the story

"The Three Bears," use a lighter breath. However, once you have differentiated the characters in any way you must be consistent throughout the story.

"Life is in the breath; therefore he who only half breathes, half lives" is a Yogic proverb storytellers should heed. The person who breathes deeply has more life, is more "alive." Yogic breathing exercises relax the body and bring vitality. Here are directions for the Complete Breath.

1. Sit in a cross-legged posture. Slowly exhale through the nose. Simultaneously contract the abdomen as far as possible to help empty all air from the lungs.
2. Slowly inhale through the nose. Simultaneously attempt to push out the abdominal area. This movement permits air being inhaled to enter the lower area of the lungs.
3. Continue the slow, quiet inhalation. Simultaneously contract the abdomen slightly and attempt to expand the chest as far as possible.
4. Continue the slow, quiet inhalation. Simultaneously raise the shoulders slowly as high as possible. This permits air to enter the high area of the lungs.
5. Hold breath with shoulders raised for a count of five.
6. Slowly and quietly exhale deeply, relaxing shoulders and chest as you exhale and contract abdomen.
7. When exhalation is completed, repeat.

Besides Yoga, there are many exercises to relax the body. Choose one that relaxes you, for example, rotate head on shoulders; relax throat by yawning; swing arms, then legs; rotate ankles. Here are two longer exercises that students find very relaxing:

1. Stand tall; raise your arms over your head; stretch high; tense every muscle. Think of yourself as a puppet on a taut string. Then, one by one, let your hands flop, bend your elbows, bring bent arms to your sides, bend forward from your waist, and hang limp with relaxed knees. Let your arms and hands dangle. Slowly come to an upright position. Repeat.
2. Lie on your back. Close your eyes and breathe slowly. Think of yourself as a rag doll filled with sawdust. Imagine that the saw-

dust is slowly seeping out of you, from toes to head. Let your whole body go limp. Remain in this position for five to ten minutes.

To overcome lazy habits of articulation, it is necessary to exercise the speech organs in much the same way that we exercise for muscular coordination in athletics or instrumental music. Regina Brown, an actress and former staff member of the New York Public Library, who for many summers worked as a storyteller in the parks and playgrounds, suggests these exercises:

*Tongue Exercises*
1. Stick out tongue and touch nose; point tongue.
2. Stick out tongue and touch chin; point tongue.
3. Stick out tongue from right side of mouth; point tongue.
4. Stick out tongue from left side of mouth; point tongue.
5. Rotate tongue—encircle lips first to right, then to left.
6. Trill tongue.
7. Repeat "Around the rugged rock the ragged rascal ran" three times.

*Lip Exercises*
1. Pout, relax; pout, relax.
2. Spread lips and say *E* (long *E*).
3. Round lips and say *OO*.

*Jaw Exercises*
1. Move jaw from side to side.
2. Move jaw up and down.
3. Rotate jaw first to left, then to right, then open and close mouth slowly.

Take time to learn your stories. Marie Shedlock advised her students to learn no more than seven stories a year. She herself learned only three stories a year, but they were learned to perfection. Don't be afraid to repeat your stories. Children enjoy hearing them again and again. Tell them at library story hours, to school classes, during visits to youth organizations. A repertoire of 20 stories of different types will serve you well.

## Learning a Folktale

1. Learn the folktale as a whole, using the "visual" approach described on pages 43–44. Do not memorize word for word.
2. Follow the steps described in the section "Basic Steps in Learning a Story," on pages 46–52.

The art of telling a folktale was, perhaps, best expressed by Mary Gould Davis in these words:

> It needs no technique to tell a folk story. What it really needs is a knowledge of literature, a thorough enjoyment of the tale, and a picture in either the mental or the physical eye of the country that the tale comes from. The greatest enemy to the successful telling of a folktale is self-consciousness. There is no self behind a folk story—there is only a slow, natural, almost inevitable growth. If we put self into it we take away from its simplicity, its frankness, its almost ruthless reality. It should be our first care to select the editor or translator who has had the courage and the wisdom to let the story reflect not his own scholarship or his power as a writer, but the country from which it comes. Every bit of knowledge that we, as storytellers, have about that country helps us.[7]

## Learning a Literary Fairy Tale

The literary fairy tales are more difficult to tell and take longer to prepare because their beauty and vitality lie in their wording, which must be retained as nearly as possible. The storyteller is interpreting a piece of creative writing. Each word and its placement in the sentence have special value and importance in relation to the story as a whole. These stories must be memorized, but the storyteller must know them so well that the artificiality and mechanization of the memorization process have been overcome. The storyteller reads and rereads the story until the memorization of it has become an unconscious one and not one of rote learning.

Reading other stories by the same author will help the storyteller discover the rhythm of the author and will reinforce perception of his or her style. Authors have a very personal way of speaking. When we hear "O Best Beloved" we immediately think of Rudyard Kipling. We recognize Laurence Housman's voice in such expressions as:

> Now anyone can see that a man who practiced so cunning a ro-
> guery was greedy beyond the intentions of Providence. . . . The
> gnome laughed to himself to see how the trapper was being
> trapped in his own avarice. . . . And now the rat-catcher was the
> richest man in the world: all his traps were made of gold, and when
> he went rat-hunting he rode in a gilded coach drawn by twelve
> hundred of the finest rats. This was for an advertisement of the
> business. He now caught rats for the fun of it and the show of it,
> but also to get money by it; for, though he was so rich, ratting and
> money-grubbing had become a second nature to him; unless he
> were at one or the other, he could not be happy.
>
> From "The Rat-Catcher's Daughter," in *The
> Rat-Catcher's Daughter: A Collection of Stories by
> Laurence Housman*, selected by Ellin Greene.[8]

About the literary fairy tale, Mary Gould Davis wrote:

> This type of story has always seemed to me very much dependent
> upon personality. If it does not kindle in us a responsive spark, if
> we do not feel that between the writer and us there is a peculiar
> understanding, then—no matter how carefully we learn it, how
> faithfully we tell it—it remains a dead thing. But when that spark is
> kindled, as instinctively, as unconsciously as the musician strikes
> the right note, we reproduce the style, the "power with words" of
> the author. We know, for instance, that it is a kind of betrayal to
> begin the story of "The Elephant's Child" with "Once Upon a
> Time." We may interest and please the children with the adven-
> tures of the young elephant and the crocodile; but, if we use that
> old traditional folk beginning, we know that we have struck the
> wrong key—we have left something out. And if we search our-
> selves thoroughly enough, we will find that the thing we have left
> out is no more and no less than Mr. Kipling! There is only one way
> in which to begin the story of "The Elephant's Child" and that is
> the way Kipling begins it—"In the High and Far Off Times, O Best
> Beloved. . . ." The quality in us that makes it possible for us to tell
> a stylist story successfully is closely akin to the quality that lets us
> read poetry successfully. A sense of rhythm and a sense of words—
> they go hand in hand. They are sister to the art of music and the art

of dancing. They are the necessary part, I think, to the art of story-telling.[9]

Knowing and enjoying other stories by the same author bring an intangible quality to the telling. Give yourself time to get to know your author. Know in October that you want to tell an Andersen story in April. Steep yourself in Andersen as you learn your story.

Memorize the literary fairy tale, then forget it has been learned word for word and tell it naturally rather than in a recitative manner. It is far better to read such stories aloud than to spoil them with inept telling.

## Should a Storyteller Who Does Not Like or Who Is Offended by Parts of a Story Adapt It?

The best thing to do is to choose another story. It will be easier to learn as well as to tell. The storyteller's adaptation often changes the meaning of the story or even mutilates it. It is unfair to the author who has researched the story, if it is a folktale, and worked hard on its creation, if it is original. Should we let a little bird warn the Gingerbread Boy so he can run home to safety or have the Fox eat him? We know the version the children prefer.

A young librarian was constantly asked by the neighborhood children in a branch of the New York Public Library to read Wanda Gág's *Millions of Cats* (Coward). One day she was ill and another librarian took her place in the reading-aloud area. The children asked her to read their favorite. When the librarian reached the part in the story where the cats fight and scratch so that only one poor little cat is left, the children all shouted, "No! That isn't the way the story goes." Questioning revealed that the first storyteller had permitted the cats to argue a bit and then run away and hide under bushes, leaving the forlorn little cat alone. When questioned, she stated that she changed that part of the story because she did not approve of violence in a children's book. The children, however, preferred the Gág version to an edited one. The librarian was strongly urged to select stories thereafter of which she approved, for storytellers must believe in and enjoy the stories they select for telling.

## How Does a Storyteller Cut a Story?

Occasionally a storyteller may wish to shorten a story because it is too long for the time allowed or the form is not best for dramatic effect or the action is slowed down by long descriptive passages. Cutting a story requires knowledge of storytelling literature and knowledge of children's reactions to hearing stories. Such knowledge comes with experience. The experienced storyteller knows what to leave out. The beginning storyteller has a tendency to cut out all description and atmosphere and to reduce the story to a mere outline. An experienced storyteller cautions, "Don't have the characters acting on an empty stage." The beginner should select a good version of a story and stick with it. Such versions may be found in recommended lists or in collections compiled by storytellers. The storyteller who has gained a sense of security will know when a small alteration in some phrase would make for smoothness, a descriptive passage might be shortened, a section might be summarized, or superfluous details and unnecessary complications of plot deleted.

In making any changes the storyteller must analyze the story and choose the most essential happenings leading to the climax. If there are two or more threads of narrative, choose one and keep it. Develop the story in a logical sequence and keep the language simple.

## How Does a Storyteller Amplify a Short Story?

The storyteller needs to flesh out the scenes and characters of a "bare-bones" story, using imagination to create vivid word pictures. The experienced storyteller is able to combine different versions of a story successfully. In doing so, it is wise to rewrite the story on paper and learn the rewritten version. Using readings of different versions of "Uncle Bouqui Rents a Horse," one storyteller began to enumerate the people on the horse rather than use Courlander's simple statement, "And they were all on the horse." This change made the telling more vivid to the children. As in cutting a story, the storyteller must keep the story whole, presenting a single point of view and developing the events in logical sequence. Ashley Bryan, in *The Cat's Purr* (Atheneum), retold an old West Indian folktale, "Why Cats Eat Rats." Bryan de-emphasizes why cats eat rats and creates a plausible origin of the cat's purr. The original folktale and its source are given in the book.

## Should an Author's or a Storyteller's Own Words Be Used?

Use the author's words if they are better than yours. Increase your own vocabulary. How many synonyms can you find for "beautiful," for "brave"? In telling stories in our own words, we often reuse the same words, especially adjectives. Be careful not to intersperse the story with "huh," "and now," and other speech mannerisms we can catch if we listen to ourselves. Respect the spare quality of such stories as those found in Joseph Jacobs's *English Fairy Tales*, and do not embellish them with your own additional words. Avoid slang when telling a traditional tale.

Are our colloquialisms appropriate to the story? The storyteller's own words should never change the meaning, the rhythm, or the cadence of a story. In telling Sandburg's "The Huckabuck Family and How They Raised Pop Corn in Nebraska and Quit and Came Back," a new storyteller changed "squash" to "pumpkin" because she thought that the children might not know "squash" pie, but that "everyone knows pumpkin pie." This showed her insensitivity to the sounds of words. She didn't realize that Sandburg, the poet, had achieved a rhythm with "squash." This is made obvious by reading the following passage out loud, as written, and then reading it substituting the word "pumpkin" for "squash."

> And this was the year Pony Pony was going to bake her first squash pie all by herself. In one corner of the corn crib, all covered over with pop corn, she had a secret, a big round squash, a fat yellow squash, a rich squash all spotted with spots of gold.
>
> From "The Huckabuck Family and How They Raised
> Pop Corn in Nebraska and Quit and Came Back,"
> in Carl Sandburg's *Rootabaga Stories*.[10]

"Squash" and "pumpkin" have an entirely different feeling—this is a sensual thing. Children do not grow linguistically or intellectually if we constantly revise downward.

## What Should a Storyteller Do about Foreign Words in a Story?

For correct pronunciation refer to a dictionary or to a resource person, such as the language specialist, on your staff.

## Should a Storyteller Tell Stories Using Dialects?

The *Random House Dictionary of the English Language* defines dialect as: "1. a variety of a language that is distinguished from other varieties of the same language by features of phonology, grammar, and vocabulary, and by its use by a group of speakers who are set off from others geographically or socially. 2. a provincial, rural, or socially distinct variety of a language that differs from the standard language, esp. when considered as substandard." Vernacular is a speech pattern that is the native language of a place or the plain variety of speech in everyday use by ordinary people. Regional vernacular is acceptable, while dialect used to indicate social or racial inferiority is offensive and misleading. An example is the plantation story published in the early 1900s. Small children, black and white, played together on the same plantation, but in the dialogue of the book the white children spoke in impeccable English while their black playmates spoke in a dialectal gibberish.

The most commonly misused dialect is the Joel Chandler Harris version of cotton-field speech, which he used in his Brer Rabbit stories to denote the lack of education and social inferiority of the slaves. Because this "made-up" speech perpetuates a stereotype and is offensive, it should not be used today.

Syncopation of speech, with its rhythmical stress, however, is part of a storyteller's interpretation. In *God's Trombones* (Viking), James Weldon Johnson said, "He [the black poet] needs to find a form that will express the racial spirit by symbols from within rather than by symbols from without—such as the mere mutilation of English spelling and pronunciation."[11] Today such writers as Lucille Clifton, Virginia Hamilton, Julius Lester, and John Steptoe have achieved a form that is larger than dialect, that flows freely, that expresses the imagery, the idioms, the humor and pathos, the unique turns of thought often found in the black person's speech. This pattern is called black English, which speech specialists claim has different rules from standard English. The difference is in the phonology or sound systems. The rules of pronunciation vary. "Going" is standard English; "gonna" is the soft slur often found in black English; "gwine" is the offensive, author-created dialect. The latter, a manufactured, literary imitation of a dialect, is sheer burlesque.

The heavy Irish dialect in the out-of-print editions of Seumas MacManus was translated by MacManus himself when he wrote *Hibernian Nights* (Macmillan). He retained the flavor of the original tales by the use of imagery, musical narrative, humor, and colloquialisms in dialogue.

Few storytellers are able to use dialect to good advantage. Ruth Sawyer told Irish stories superbly because she had been imbued with the richness of the Irish tongue from early childhood by an Irish nurse. This same great storyteller, however, once told a German folktale in a German dialect, saying "vy" instead of "why," and "vhat" instead of "what." It did not sound natural, and the audience was embarrassed. Much practice is required to capture dialect and use it in a relaxed and comfortable manner. It is better in most cases, therefore, to avoid dialect and, instead, retain the rich expressions, the cadence, the flavor, and the inflection of the particular speech patterns.

Regional vernacular is not only acceptable but often necessary in storytelling. For example, in telling the story "Wicked John and the Devil," from Richard Chase's *Grandfather Tales* (Houghton), the storyteller must refer to "sweet milk" rather than "milk," because the former places the story geographically. As a matter of fact, the author of this story once pointed out to his audience that in Appalachia the person asking for milk rather than "sweet milk" might be served buttermilk!

## After a Storyteller Has Worked on a Story for Some Time, How Is Boredom Overcome?

There seems to be a point in the learning process when a plateau is reached and all effort is drudgery. Accept this and let the story go for a few days or a week, then return to it. Recall the emotions the story originally aroused in you. When you tell the story to children and you see the wonder in their faces or the laughter in their eyes you will feel that all the time spent on learning it was worthwhile.

## Notes

1. Sorche Nic Leodhas, "The Woman Who Flummoxed the Fairies," in Leodhas, *Heather and Broom: Tales of the Scottish Highlands* (New York: Holt, 1960), pp. 35–43.
2. Jakob and Wilhelm Grimm, "The Frog Prince," in *Tales from Grimm*, trans. by Wanda Gág (New York: Coward, 1936), pp. 179–188.
3. Laurence Housman, "The Wooing of the Maze," in *The Rat-Catcher's Daughter: A Collection of Stories by Laurence Housman*, selected by Ellin Greene (New York: Atheneum, 1974), p. 59.
4. Joseph Jacobs, "Mr. Fox," in Jacobs, *English Fairy Tales* (New York: Dover, 1898), p. 154.
5. Charles J. Finger, "The Magic Ball," in Finger, *Tales from Silver Lands* (New York: Doubleday, 1924), p. 45.
6. Eulalie Steinmetz Ross, in a manuscript in the files of the Office of Children's Services, New York Public Library. Appears in slightly altered form in *The Lost Half-Hour: A Collection of Stories*, ed. by Eulalie Steinmetz Ross (New York: Harcourt, 1963).
7. Mary Gould Davis, "The Art of Storytelling" (paper delivered at a meeting of the American Library Association, Washington, D.C., May 15, 1929).
8. Laurence Housman, "The Rat-Catcher's Daughter," in *The Rat-Catcher's Daughter: A Collection of Stories by Laurence Housman*, pp. 3, 5, 6–7.
9. Davis, "The Art of Storytelling."
10. Carl Sandburg, "The Huckabuck Family and How They Raised Pop Corn in Nebraska and Quit and Came Back," in Sandburg, *Rootabaga Stories* (New York: Harcourt, 1951), pp. 170, 173.
11. James Weldon Johnson, *God's Trombones* (New York: Viking, 1927), p. 8.

## Titles Referred to in This Chapter

Bryan, Ashley. *The Cat's Purr*. New York: Atheneum, 1985.
Chase, Richard. *Grandfather Tales*. New York: Houghton, 1948.
Gág, Wanda. *Millions of Cats*. New York: Coward, 1928, 1977.
Jacobs, Joseph. *English Fairy Tales*. New York: Dover, 1898.
MacManus, Seumas. *Hibernian Nights*. New York: Macmillan, 1963, o.p.

The authors wish to call to the reader's attention the article, " 'A Peculiar Understanding': Re-creating the Literary Fairy Tale," by Ellin Greene, published in the June 1983 issue of *Horn Book Magazine* (volume 59, number 3, pp. 270–278, 378) and reprinted in the Summer 1985 issue of *The National Storytelling Journal* (volume 2, number 3, pp. 3–6).

# 5 Presentation

A small boy sat between two adults at the village soda fountain. He had just been collected from his first library story hour, and a celebration was in order. The storyteller sat three stools away, unrecognizable in winter scarf and hood. The curious adults were trying in vain to pry some statement of reaction to the story hour from the boy, a most reluctant informer, until at last one of them complained with some asperity, "You could at least tell us how the teacher told the stories? Did she read them from a book? Did she tell them from memory?" "Oh, mother," he explained with a long sigh, "she just told them from herself."[1]

No storyteller ever received higher praise, for the ultimate goal is to tell a story so simply and directly that it appears to be told "from yourself." All the emphasis should be placed upon the story rather than upon the storyteller, who is, for the time being, simply a vehicle through which the beauty and wisdom and humor of the story come to the listener.

## Telling the Story

Before beginning, call up the essential emotions of the story as you first felt them. Breathe deeply and begin. No matter what the opening words of the story are, the tone should be intimate.

Look directly at your listeners. As you tell, let your gaze move from one to another so that each child feels involved in the telling of the story. Break direct eye contact only to look at an imaginary scene or object you want your listeners to see, or when you engage in dialogue between two or more characters during the telling.

Speak in a pleasant, low-pitched voice with enough volume to be heard easily by listeners in the last row. Speak clearly, distinctly, smoothly, and at a pace suitable for the story.

Gestures, if used at all, should be natural to the teller and to the action of the story. If gestures draw attention to themselves

FIGURE 5. Augusta Baker telling stories to children at Seminole Elementary School, Columbia, South Carolina, as part of the Artists-in-Schools Program. (Photograph © Terry L. Megehee.)

they are wrong. Exaggerated gestures usually indicate a futile attempt to draw attention away from inadequate preparation. Do not stand motionless as if you were a stick of wood, but do not dramatize the action of the story, for example, "marching up and down the road," "bowing," and so forth. The children may be fascinated with your movement, but they will not remember your story.

Use your hands naturally. Don't jam them in your pockets. Don't stand with arms crossed in a hostile posture. If you do not know what to do with your hands, hold them behind your back. "Keep your listeners in the *what* of the story, not in the how of the telling," advises an experienced storyteller.

The storyteller establishes the mood of the story hour. Physical appearance, a pleasant expression, a smile, personal warmth, pleasure in the story all give a sense of enjoyment. (Figure 5.)

Sometimes new storytellers wonder what to wear. Dress comfortably and simply. Children appreciate a bright scarf or attractive jewelry, but nothing should distract from the story. In a large hall, wearing something colorful will focus attention on the storyteller. However, there is no need to wear a "costume." Beware of jangly bracelets, long beads, and other potential distractions. One well-known storyteller wore long strands of beads. She always asked that she be reminded to remove them before the story hour. Otherwise she would begin to handle them during her telling, and the children would be as interested in whether the beads would break as they would be in the story.

A story hour can be held anywhere. Lack of a separate room is no excuse for not having a storytelling program. What is needed is a setting that is informal and an atmosphere that is relaxed and intimate. In the classroom, children may remain in their regular assigned seats, but an informal seating arrangement is preferred. A semicircle of listeners facing the storyteller seems to be the most effective arrangement. The storyteller can be heard and seen easily by all the children. Do not let the semicircle be too wide, or the storyteller's head will have to turn from side to side like a spectator's at a tennis match. If there are twenty-eight children in the group, it is better to have four rows of seven chairs than two rows of fourteen chairs. Seat the children on chairs or on the floor so that no child is directly behind another. The children should face away from the sunlight or any windows where traffic or other distractions may divert their interest. The story-teller will sit or stand, depending on the size of the group and visibility. It may be more comfortable to sit when telling to a small group or to younger children, but standing gives better eye span and, therefore, better control. It also gives the storyteller freedom of movement. If the storyteller is comfortable and confident, the children will be too. The arrangement of storyteller and listeners in Figure 6 will permit everyone to see and hear the storyteller easily.

Ask the children to put aside anything they are carrying (books, marbles, purses, dolls, and so on) on a separate table or under their chairs. If they have books in hand, they will surely peek into them during the storytelling. They really are not disin-terested in your telling, but many children can focus on two

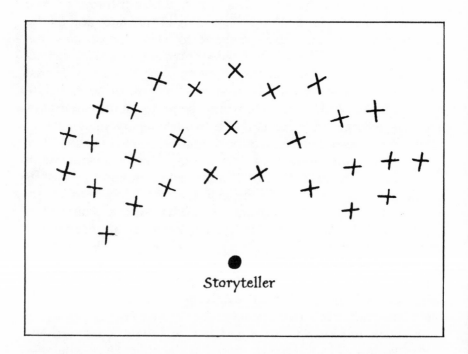

FIGURE 6. Seating arrangement for a story hour.

things at once. This can deflate you as a storyteller, and it may distract other listeners.

If there is a separate story-hour room, check the heat and ventilation before the program begins. A room that is too warm and without sufficient air will make children drowsy.

If there is no separate story-hour room, a screen can be used to give a sense of privacy. Locate the storytelling area away from room traffic, circulation desk, and telephone.

On the "story-hour" table have the books from which you are telling, some fresh or dried flowers or leaves, and, if you like, the wishing candle and realia related to the stories.

Introduce the book from which the story is taken. This can be done naturally by picking up the book, either before or after the story, and saying, "This story is from. . . ." All children, whether or not they are readers, like to hear a good story well told. After they have heard it, book-loving children want to read it again for themselves. Even girls and boys who are not natural readers will turn to a book once it has been "opened" for them by the warmth and intimacy of a storyteller's voice and personality.

No explanations of the story are necessary. Occasionally the storyteller may wish to give a short introduction. Some books, such as Eleanor Farjeon's *The Little Bookroom* (Godine), Howard Pyle's *The Wonder Clock* (Harper), and Harold Courlander's *Uncle Bouqui of Haiti* (Morrow), have natural introductions. Introductions should be interesting and simple. You are not giving a lesson. You can develop your own short introduction, for example, "In Haiti there are two very important men. One is named Bouqui and he is a fat, good-natured fellow. The other is his best friend, Ti-Malice, a skinny little fellow who always tricks Bouqui. One time, Bouqui. . . ." And then go straight into the story. The ages of your listeners will determine the type and extent of your introduction. If you are telling a long story serially, prepare a short summary to refresh the children's memory and to introduce the story to newcomers. If you tell one incident from a long book, briefly introduce the characters and the situation in which they find themselves.

No definitions of "strange" words are necessary. Frequently, inexperienced storytellers feel that they must define all unfamiliar words in order for children to understand the story. They forget that the context of the story and the child's imagination are enough to supply definitions. If children do not understand a word, they will ask, or if they look puzzled, and understanding the word is essential for meaning, the storyteller can substitute a synonym the next time the word is used in the story. For example, if the storyteller is telling "The Squire's Bride" and realizes that the children do not know what a bay mare is, the storyteller can substitute the word "horse" in the following sentence: "Some pulled at the head and the forelegs of the mare (horse) and others pushed from behind, and at last they got her up the stairs and into the room."

Then there are words that give atmosphere, and it really doesn't matter what they mean. In her delightful article "The Pleasant Land of Counterpane," Claudia Lewis recalls her childhood encounter with Robert Louis Stevenson's poem "The Land of Counterpane."

> [The poem was] magical simply because of that bewildering word counterpane. Yes, of course, my mother explained to me what it meant, and in some rational part of my mind I know very clearly what it meant. Yet it was not a word current in the everyday speech of the people around me; and it suggested a baffling combination of windowpane and kitchen counter. At the same time, what a splendid-sounding word it was! I must have closed off that rational corner of mine and let my thoughts go romping off with whatever textural images and associations the word called up, and fortunately for me, my mother did not drill in the meaning. I was left to enjoy the poem, and enjoy it I did, in my own way. It would be difficult for me to describe just what "the pleasant land of counterpane" was to me (and still is). This is a case of the quality of a particular word spilling over and giving color to a whole poem, or rather, to the poem one reconstructs inwardly in heightened imaginative dimensions.[2]

If a storyteller becomes bogged down in a vocabulary lesson the pleasure is diminished for the children, who should be allowed to relax and enjoy the story.

In planning a satisfying story hour, the storyteller must be concerned with a variety of practical problems as well as with the content. Some of these concerns are reflected in the following questions.

## Should the Story-Hour Group Be Large or Small?

When no visuals are used there are no restrictions as to size. However, a group of from 20 to 30 children is a comfortable size, especially for the beginning storyteller. Experience brings the ability to project to large groups. If you anticipate frequent story hours to large groups or storytelling out-of-doors, you will need to develop your voice so that you can project it without distorting the quality.

Occasionally, the storyteller is asked to tell stories at a school assembly. Although this can be done effectively, it is difficult to create an intimate "from me to you" feeling in an assembly setting. If you have this type of request, you might ask if it would be possible to tell to several smaller groups of children rather than to a large assembly. Though telling to several groups on the same day may be physically more demanding of the storyteller, it makes for more satisfying story hours.

## How Is a Listening Mood Created?

The mood is created by attractive surroundings—a well-ventilated room, comfortable seating, the story-hour table with appropriate, authentic realia, clean books, some fresh flowers or leaves, and the wishing candle, if it is to be used. The rituals of the story-hour line and the wishing candle also help to establish a listening mood. However, it is the storyteller who is most important in setting the mood. The storyteller's manner should be dignified but friendly. It should say, "Listen deeply, for I have something special to share with you."

## What Is the Story-Hour Line and What Are Its Advantages?

The story-hour line can be used wherever there is a separate storytelling area. Have the children assemble in a line away from the story-hour area. This gives the children a chance to quiet down before entering the story hour. It gives the storyteller a chance to assess the group. This is the time to ask the children to

FIGURE 7. A storytelling hour at the Chatham Square branch of the New York Public Library. Augusta Baker, former N.Y.P.L. Coordinator of Children's Services, lights the wishing candle. (Photograph courtesy of the New York Public Library.)

put away gum, candy, toys, and anything else that might divert them from listening.

The formality is liked by children and makes for a mood of wonder, as described in this excerpt from the psychoanalysis of a 24-year-old woman, who recalled going to story hour when she was about 7 years old:

> This just reminded me of my greatest happiness and excitement as a child. And that was going every Friday afternoon after school to storytelling in the Public Library. It was not just ordinary storytelling. First, all of the children lined up and waited. . . . Then they led us down into a room in the cellar with chairs all arranged in rows. The room had the most immense and useless windows you ever saw. Not only were they completely out of reach, but the shades were always drawn tight so that the room was dark except for the glow of two immense candles on a desk at the front. And behind the desk, illuminated by the candlelight, was the prettiest face imaginable. I am quite sure there was a body attached to the face. But I do not remember it. She must have been the librarian . . . but then I never thought of her as being a mere librarian any more than a child can conceive of its mother as a little baby. She was a real fairy that came to tell us stories. I loved the first story best always because there were two more to come. I hated, hated, hated, having to go upstairs when all the stories were done.[3]

## How Is the Wishing Candle Used?

The lighting of the candle helps to create a mood and indicates the start of the program. Before lighting the candle, the storyteller may say, "Once the candle is lit, no one speaks but the storyteller." Wishes are made silently at the end of the story hour, and the seated children blow out the candle, which is held by the storyteller, or one child—perhaps a birthday child—may be chosen to blow out the candle while everyone makes silent wishes. Be sure to use a dripless candle to avoid being sprayed with wax when the candle is blown out! (Figure 7.)

## Does the Presentation of a Story Differ When It Is Told to Different Age Groups?

In telling to different age groups the storyteller's facial expressions or attitude or approach to the story may be different. The listeners play an important role. Children will be responding to the story line, adults and older children to the subtle humor or poignancy of a tale. The subtle interplay between husband and wife in "Two of Everything" is lost on children but not on adults. In telling "Uncle Bouqui Rents a Horse" the last sentence, "This *certainly is a day* ever to remember," when told to adults, is said with a sarcastic inflection. Of course there are many stories that can be told successfully to different age groups without changing the presentation. "Mr. Sampson Cat" is one of them.

## How Can a Storyteller Tell If the Children Are Enjoying the Story?

When children are enjoying a story their faces express interest, curiosity, delight. Sometimes their pleasure is expressed by listening quietly with little or no expression on their faces. A deep sigh and a faraway look at the end of the story usually mean that you have reached that child. Some children do not seem to be paying attention at all; yet these same children will ask you for the story several weeks after you have told it. The new storyteller must remember that a story that is a roaring success with one group can leave another cold. Do not be discouraged. Continue to work on any story you really like. Accept failure along with your successes.

## What Does a Storyteller Do If the Children Seem to Be Disinterested or Not in the Mood to Listen to a Particular Tale?

An element of flexibility is needed. Restlessness often occurs when the story chosen is a poor one for the group or when the storyteller has failed to capture the imagination of the children at the beginning. Sometimes the storyteller can recapture the children's interest by telling with greater conviction. However, if this fails, it is best to summarize the remaining part of the story and bring the story hour to a close or, if possible, tell a different type of story. The story hour should be remembered with joy.

## What Is the Best Way to Handle Disruptions?

The storyteller must be aware of the audience. Because the storyteller respects both story and listeners, no one should be allowed to disrupt what promises to be an enjoyable listening experience. Do not permit two little girls who are giggling and whispering to each other to sit together. They will surely whisper in the middle of the story even though they are following it closely.

Weave discipline into your telling. For example, in coping with restless listeners, you might insert as part of your story, "You two boys in the back could never guess. . . ." One storyteller, who was telling a story about a beautiful princess, used this ploy with "success" beyond her expectations. As she told her story she looked directly at a little girl who was chewing bubble gum and interjected, "And the princess did not chew gum." The girl was so surprised she swallowed her gum!

The following example may be helpful in handling a difficult situation: As you start to tell the story you are aware that Johnny is surreptitiously punching Willy. For a few seconds you tell the story directly to him. Your tone of voice is firm. You look away in order to give the boys a chance to behave, but they continue to punch each other. Now they are challenging you. As you continue the story, you take a few steps toward them. Your tone of voice and body language are clearly understood by the boys. You move away again and continue the story. The third time they misbehave, you stop the story and tell them they will have to leave if they continue to disrupt the story hour. You apologize to the other children that this has happened, then go on with the story. If the two boys do not settle down, you ask them to leave. The storyteller has a responsibility to the group and cannot let a few children spoil the story hour.

## What Should Storytellers Do If They Forget the Story?

Because the book from which you are telling your story will be close by on the story-hour table, place a small marker in the first page of your story. If you forget your story, pick up the book and open it to the marker, which will guide you to your story. Without it you will search nervously through the book and lose your poise. Many times a glance at the place in the story where you forgot will set you free again, and you can put the book back on the table. If not, *read* the rest of the story. More often than not, if you know the story well and you have a moment of forgetfulness, you can improvise until the story comes back to you. If you forget an essential part of the story say, "Did I tell you that . . ." rather than, "Oh, I forgot to tell you that. . . ."

## How Does a Storyteller Conclude the Story Hour?

End with the ending of the story. When the story is over, its spirit remains. Honor the story with a minute or two of silence (Marie Shedlock recommended five minutes of complete silence after a story). Do not ask questions about the story or try to elicit comments. Let the children leave the story hour with their own private thoughts. Do not invade their privacy. After the few minutes of silence, a simple "Thank you for coming," not a corny "We have been down the road to fairyland," is a good conclusion to the story hour held in the public library or recreation center. Now is the time to announce the next story hour. Collect story-hour tickets if you have not done so already. Direct the children to books. Let the children go two or three at a time in order to avoid disrupting other areas of the library. Be available after the story hour to discuss stories with those children who take the initiative, who *want* to talk.

## Should There Be Follow-Up Activities after the Story?

Any follow-up activity should have a close relationship to the theme of the story. An activity that deepens a child's appreciation of the story is appropriate, but too often activities are tacked on to provide a learning experience. To tell the story "The Blind Boy and the Loon" and then to have the children construct igloos of flour and salt or to talk about the coloration of the loon is not what the story is about. Having the children dramatize the story might have a relationship. The best way, usually, is simply to pause after the story and then go on to the next activity of the day.

## What Are the Qualities of a Good Storyteller?

The early storytellers had qualities that are just as important today. One must have a keen enjoyment of one's material and a burning desire to share one's enthusiasm with others. Elizabeth Nesbitt, a storyteller long associated with the Carnegie Library of Pittsburgh, said:

Storytelling, like anything else, cannot achieve its rightful best unless it is done with understanding, integrity, and acceptance of the
fact that it requires thought, care, time, and knowledge in selection
and preparation, and recognition of the necessity for a special kind
of artistry in the telling. The art of storytelling is a spontaneous, un-
sophisticated art.[4]

It holds, therefore, that storytelling is an individual art, and
that each storyteller will bring a special kind of appreciation,
imagination, and interpretation to the telling. Extensive reading
and building of background are necessary, for the storyteller must
think of the story as a part of the whole literature to which it be-
longs and of the storyteller as the medium through which the
story comes to life.

All creative artists share the same qualities—enthusiasm,
spontaneity, imagination, perception, insight. A good storyteller
is also a vital human being who finds joy in living, and who can
reach the heart and mind of a child. Taste and appreciation grow
as the storyteller is exposed to art, to music, and to dance; the
entire range of feelings, intellect, and spirit comes alive. Good
storytellers, like good wine, age well. The words of the story may
not change, but what the storyteller brings to the story changes
with the experience of living.

Children demand the best, and they walk away from anything less. Good storytelling presupposes a willingness to work
hard. In "Storytelling—A Folk Art," a chapter in *The Way of the
Storyteller*, Ruth Sawyer says that she has no basic recipe for good
storytelling. The most important requirement for her is the right
approach and the recognition that storytelling is a folk art. She
does, however, list certain invariables—experience, building of
background, creative imagination, and a gift for selection.

Marie Shedlock had these qualities, as have other great storytellers. Ruth Sawyer was inspired by Miss Shedlock and remembers:

The qualities that Miss Shedlock brought to her art, and of which
she gave so abundantly to all who listened, have remained for us
the high mark of perfect storytelling. Voice and the spoken word
were the medium for the art, and she used them with that same
care and appreciation with which a painter uses line, color, and

perspective. She had a wonderful voice, perfectly pitched, flexible. She never droned. Her sense of timing was always right: she knew the value of a pause. Her power to build expectation as the story grew combined both the traditional art and that of the conscious and trained artist. She belonged to those stories she told as the traditional storyteller belonged to those which had been handed down to him, an enduring legacy. Everyone who remembers her telling of the fairy tales of Hans Christian Andersen knows how deeply rooted was this kinship.[5]

## What Is the Difference between a Performer-Storyteller and a Librarian/Teacher-Storyteller?

In the current renaissance of storytelling the subtle line between performance and telling is becoming increasingly hard to define. Constance A. Mellon, director of the National Clearinghouse for Information on Storytelling (NCIS), suggests that the difference lies in the relationship between the teller and the listener. "And the focus of that relationship is the story."[6]

Performer-storytellers have a dramatic style. Usually they have had some theatrical and voice training, have stage presence, and enjoy being "on stage" and telling to a large audience. Mary Gould Davis called the librarian/teacher-storyteller who enjoys telling stories to children but who does not like to give a performance "the children's storyteller." She wrote, regarding the two types of storytellers:

> Almost anyone who knows and loves a good tale . . . can tell it effectively to a small, intimate group. To make a story effective to a large group in a more or less formal atmosphere requires what Marie Shedlock calls "the art of the storyteller": an interpretive art as subtle and as challenging as that of the musician or the painter. To broaden and to perfect this art one can give years of study and comparison, of travel to the countries from which the stories come. One can study the latent possibilities of the human voice, inflection, emphasis, the use of the pause. But, because in the minds of the children the important thing is not the storyteller but the *story*, one can, with no training nor experience whatsoever, take the *right* book, tell the *right* tale and hold the boys and girls in a "listening silence."[7]

More recently, Kay Stone wrote in the same vein:

As with a traditional audience, children are not passive listeners, and they still live in a predominantly oral milieu. They do not demand a flamboyantly oral/visual performance (though many adults think it necessary). They do demand sincerity and openness, and they tend to suffer honest fools gladly. Like a traditional audience they do not stop to ask, "Was that profound and meaningful, or just amusing?" If a story is well-told, they will absorb other levels of meaning that appeal to their levels of experience and understanding.[8]

Stories may be interpreted in many ways. All that matters is that the style fit the teller. Two students told "Tom Tit Tot." One imbued the story with mystery and all kinds of psychological implications. The other told the tale as if she were the "gatless" young girl herself. Both tellings were successful because they were appropriate for the story and for the teller.

## What Is the Difference between Telling a Story to an Individual Child at Home and Telling a Story to a Group of Children?

The adult telling a story to an individual child at home is very much aware of that child's interests, fears, likes, and dislikes. This knowledge makes it easier to choose a story that will appeal. The telling is informal and interruptions are permitted since there is no time schedule to keep. Telling to a group of children is more formal—the larger the group, the more formal the presentation, usually, but there are exceptions, such as storytelling around a camp fire. The storyteller does not expect every child in the group to have the same listening experience or to like the tale equally well.

It would not be appropriate to tell a story to one or two children in exactly the same manner that it would be told to a group of children. The experience might be too intense, too emotionally demanding of the child. In a group, a child is freer to let his or her mind engage in imaginative play.

## Is There a Place for Spontaneous Storytelling?

Storytelling should not be limited to the scheduled story hour. If you are prepared and an opportunity presents itself, such as a quiet day in the public library, at school when a story would relate naturally to the classroom discussion, or at the end of an activity when the children need a change of pace, tell a story or read aloud.

## What Are the Values of Reading Aloud?

Reading aloud is a potent means for influencing the reading tastes of children. Reading good books aloud can introduce them to those they might miss, can reinforce old favorites, and can give them a standard for measuring books in the future. Reading aloud is an educational tool as well as an instrument of culture. As an educational tool, reading aloud is an aid to greater accuracy and better understanding of the written word. A story read with enjoyment is not a reading exercise. Rather, it is an auditory experience, as is storytelling, and listeners learn to associate reading with pleasure. They become familiar with much of the choice literature that is common to our culture. The rhythm of language, both poetry and prose, is best appreciated through auditory experience. Children may come to realize that reading is the key to wealth that they can gain for themselves through books. Reading and listening are the receptive arts, just as speaking (telling) and writing are the expressive arts. Reading aloud does for a literate society what the telling of folktales does for a folk society.

## What Are the Two Main Purposes of Reading Aloud?

Reading aloud may be utilitarian or interpretive. The former is the secretary reading the minutes of a meeting or a person reading aloud a news item. The interpretive purpose is also communicative, but it differs from the utilitarian in being less objective and in being concerned with the communication of something more than information. The reader wants to share with others his or her appreciation of the book and the emotional experience derived from it.

## What Should Be Read Aloud?

Do not waste your time and the children's time by reading ordinary, dull, uninspiring, vocabulary-controlled stories. Select books and stories of literary merit that may be a little beyond the reading ability of the listeners—they can listen and perhaps be motivated to grow in their ability to read. Read only what you enjoy, so that your enjoyment is transferred to the listeners. One of the main purposes in reading aloud is to give the listeners a pleasurable experience.

The length of the material should be suitable to the maturity of the group. It is best to choose stories that can be read in one sitting if the children are young or if you find yourself with a different group of children each time you read, as often happens in a public library. Whole books can be read as serials, a chapter or two at a time. Myths, legends, hero tales, and tall tales lend themselves well to reading aloud. Poetry almost demands to be read aloud. Reading a poem aloud catches elements that are missed when it is read silently.

Two excellent sources of titles to read aloud, from picture books to full-length fiction, can be found in *For Reading Out Loud! A Guide to Sharing Books with Children*, by Margaret Mary Kimmel and Elizabeth Segel (Delacorte), and *The Read-Aloud Handbook*, by Jim Trelease (Viking Penguin).

## Is There an Art to Reading Aloud?

Reading aloud is an art and, like storytelling, requires practice to be effective. The art is many faceted. Because the main thrust of interpretive reading is one of enjoyment and not teaching, the mood should be one of relaxed listening. Do not invade the privacy of a child's thoughts by forcing comments. Do not read in a condescending manner. And do have a sense of humor. Know your material so well that you do not struggle over words and ideas and can look frequently at your listeners in order to involve them in the story. Strengthen your technical equipment—pleasant, flexible voice, clear enunciation, skillful pacing that captures the rhythms and conveys the mood. The timing and the pause are as important in reading aloud as in storytelling. This is storytelling with the book.

Read in a natural voice but with expression and feeling. Styles have changed in interpretive reading, and elocution, declamations, and automatic recitation are things of the past. Today, reading aloud is divorced from dramatic acting, impersonation, or exhibitionism, and the fullness of one's appreciation can be reflected in a rich expressiveness of voice and manner. The reader appreciates, interprets, and calls attention to what the author has created with as much imaginative skill as possible.

## Is Storytelling More Important Than Reading Aloud?

Both experiences are important to create and sustain children's interest in books and reading. However, the teller, unhampered by the necessity of reading from a book, is able to communicate more fully with the listeners by using eye contact. Beginning storytellers who use reading aloud as a security blanket are encouraged to try telling without a book. They will find the experience exhilarating.

## Notes

1. Eulalie Steinmetz Ross, manuscript in the files of the Office of Children's Services, New York Public Library.
2. Claudia Lewis, "The Pleasant Land of Counterpane," *Horn Book Magazine*, October 1966, p. 543.
3. From the personal files of Augusta Baker.
4. Elizabeth Nesbitt, "The Art of Storytelling," *Catholic Library World* 34 (November 1962): 143–145.
5. Ruth Sawyer, "Storytelling: Fifty Years A-growing," in *Reading without Boundaries*, ed. by Frances Lander Spain (New York: New York Public Library, 1956), p. 61.
6. Constance A. Mellon, "Storyteller or Performer? You Can't Tell the Difference without a Scorecard," *School Library Journal*, October 1986, p. 122. Excerpted from *By Word of Mouth* (vol. 1, no. 1) Winter 1986.
7. Mary Gould Davis, "The Art of Storytelling" (paper presented at a meeting of the American Library Association, Washington, D.C., May 15, 1929).
8. Kay Stone, "'To Ease the Heart': Traditional Storytelling," *National Storytelling Journal*, Winter 1984, p. 5.

## Titles Referred to in This Chapter

Courlander, Harold. *Uncle Bouqui of Haiti.* New York: Morrow, 1942, o.p.
Farjeon, Eleanor. *The Little Bookroom.* New York: Walck, 1956, o.p.; Boston: Godine, 1984.
Kimmel, Margaret Mary, and Segel, Elizabeth. *For Reading Out Loud! A Guide to Sharing Books with Children.* New York: Delacorte, 1983.

Pyle, Howard. *The Wonder Clock.* New York: Harper, 1887; New York: Dover, 1965.

Sawyer, Ruth. *The Way of the Storyteller.* New York: Viking, 1942; rev. ed. Baltimore: Penguin, 1977.

Trelease, Jim. *The Read-Aloud Handbook,* rev. ed. New York: Viking Penguin, 1985.

# 6 Storytelling in Special Settings or to Children with Special Needs

There is very little in library or education literature to help the storyteller who tells to children with special needs—the mentally retarded, the blind and partially sighted, the deaf and other physically handicapped, the physically ill, the emotionally disturbed. Mainstreaming means that many more of these children will be included in regular story-hour groups. Mainstreaming has extended our awareness of their needs, but courses in the skills needed for effective storytelling to these children are offered rarely. Various age groups, such as infants and toddlers, and teenagers also have special needs of which the storyteller needs to be aware.

The storyteller who tells to children with special needs must have the qualities of a good storyteller, only more so. Extra warmth and extra sensitivity to the group's needs are necessary in order to sustain good listening. Each child must be seen not as handicapped, but as a child with a handicap, that is, the emphasis must be on the *whole* child. (Figure 8.)

"Storytelling to children with special needs is a joy and a challenge," writes Louise M. Pulley, Special Services for Special Children, Forsyth County Public Library System, North Carolina. She continues:

> The storyteller will find that there is a greater need to use facial and vocal expression, body language and animation to get and hold the attention of the children. Use visuals, such as flannelboard stories, finger puppets, story dolls, and other realia. Flannelboard stories are very successful due to the simplicity of the patterns, ease of movement and clarity of story. Be sure the pictures are large enough to be seen by the entire group and sturdy enough for repeated handling. Make the pieces move by "walking" them across the board, moving them to match the action of the story, and re-

FIGURE 8. Whatever their physical or mental limitations, children and young people enjoy a tale. Spencer Shaw telling stories at the Special Human Resources School, Albertson, Long Island, New York. (Photograph © George E. Ernst.)

moving them as soon as they are not needed. Use the fewest pieces possible for the storyline to avoid confusion of multiple changes. Know the story well, have all pieces in the order they are to be used. Children love the sequential stories, one character building on the others as in "Henny Penny," "Gingerbread Boy," etc. Get the children to name the characters with you, join in the repetitive phrases, repeat the sing-song storyline!

The following brief suggestions are offered to the storyteller who has had little or no experience in this area. Additional suggestions can be found in ALSC Program Support Publication Number 2, "Programming for Children with Special Needs," prepared by the American Library Association Library Service to Children with Special Needs Committee (ALA), and *The Special Child in the Library*, by Barbara Holland Baskin and Karen H. Harris (ALA). The reader is also encouraged to read *Cushla and Her Books*, by Dorothy Butler (Horn Book). This is a loving account of the remarkable role stories played in the early development of a multiple-disabled child.

### Storytelling to Blind or Partially Sighted Children

Storytelling is done much as it is for children with sight. However, because facial expressions and body movement are lost on the listeners, the storyteller's choice of words and voice quality are extremely important. A pleasing, musical voice is a great asset to all storytellers, but it is vital for the storyteller who tells to blind children. For blind children, beauty of language comes through the sound.

Storytelling is important to blind children for language development. Choose stories with vivid mental images. Craig Werner, now a teacher of children's literature, writes that the stories he enjoyed most as a child were those he could perceive through tactile means, that is, stories with long descriptive passages, such as the fairy tales of Hans Christian Andersen. He concludes that *imagination* is the most important faculty involved in understanding and appreciating a good story.[1]

Fine filmstrips, such as those produced by Weston Woods, can be used successfully with partially sighted children.

## Storytelling to Mentally Retarded Children

Mentally retarded children tend to be even more literal-minded than most children. They enjoy simple stories about animals and familiar things. Look for strong plot, obvious humor, simple vocabulary, and concrete language rather than abstractions. Be prepared to substitute synonyms for unfamiliar words. Use pictures and realia to illustrate unfamiliar words.

Choose picture-book stories in which the pictures tell the story. Bruno Munari's story *The Birthday Present* (World) has sure-fire appeal. Mark, the truck driver, is taking a birthday present to his little boy, John. When his truck breaks down, he must find other means of transportation. The unusual format of the book, the simple story line, the various and familiar means of transportation, and the adult male main character give this book special appeal.

The tight structure of the folktale, with its definite beginning, middle, and ending, is particularly satisfying to these children, and cumulative folktales (see Appendix 3) are enjoyed as much for their repetition and rhythm as for their plot. Participation stories are also popular. Having the children retell the story in another form, for example, through creative drama or dance, reinforces the story.

## Storytelling to Learning Disabled Children

Learning disabled children often exhibit disorders in listening, speaking, and thinking processes. Other characteristics include disorientation, distractibility, disorganization, and a limited attention span. Brevity and concreteness in the selection of stories for this group have been advised in the past. However, Jed Luchow, a teacher of young learning disabled children, found that unity "expressed in oneness of mood, plot, character, harmony between picture and story, or harmony between picture and detail" is more relevant.[2] Some of the books Luchow found to be enjoyed by the children are *Mike Mulligan and His Steam Shovel*, by Virginia Lee Burton (Houghton), *Whistle for Willie*, by Ezra Jack Keats (Viking), and *Where the Wild Things Are*, by Maurice Sendak (Harper).

## Storytelling to Emotionally Disturbed Children

Emotionally disturbed children tend toward hyperactivity, impulsiveness, and anxiety. These children usually have a very short attention span. Tell stories that have quiet humor. Tell more slowly. Involve the children in the telling. *Listen and Help Tell the Story*, by Bernice Wells Carlson (Abingdon), contains a great deal of material that can be used effectively.

## Storytelling to Children with Impaired Hearing

Telling stories to children with impaired hearing requires very special techniques. The visual presentation provides the meaning.

Sit or stand so that your back is to the light, putting your face in shadow so that you can be seen more easily.

Make use of facial expressions and body movement.

Speak more slowly and in a moderate tone of voice, but do not mouth each word, as this distorts the normal rhythm. A lip-reader is looking for the thought, not single words. Women story-tellers should be aware that lips are more visible if lipstick is worn. Men storytellers should remember that lips can be read more easily if there is no mustache or beard.

Repeat the thought, express it in different words to make the thought clear. Repeat, paraphrase, and rephrase what is being said. Beauty of language to children whose hearing is impaired is a matter of understanding the meaning of words.

In terms of language understanding, these children are often two to three years behind children whose hearing is not impaired. For example, folktales and fairy tales for the hearing child of age 8 or 9 may not be appropriate for the nonhearing child until age 10 or 11.

It is sometimes necessary to adapt the story drastically, something not recommended when telling to a hearing person. Use short simple sentences and a direct style. Picture-book editions are good if the pictures are clear and really tell the story, as in Grimm's *The Shoemaker and the Elves*, illustrated by Adrienne Adams (Scribner).

Choose stories with action and humor, such as *Mr. Gumpy's*

*Outing,* by John Burningham (Holt), and *The Very Hungry Caterpillar,* by Eric Carle (Philomel).

Children with impaired hearing cannot use their eyes and ears simultaneously. They cannot look at pictures and read your lips or signing at the same time. Close the book as you tell (contrary to the usual way of holding a picture book open with the pages turned toward the children as the storyteller reads aloud). Then open the book to show the pictures.

Hearing and nonhearing children can enjoy stories together with the assistance of a sign storyteller. The storyteller tells the story slowly and watches the person signing to make sure they are together.

Children with hearing problems usually tire more quickly when they are required to pay close attention to looking or listening. Extra concentration is called for; therefore, one story—or two short stories—is usually sufficient for the storytelling period.

## Storytelling to Children in Hospitals

Time passes slowly for the hospitalized child. The stay may be short or it may be several weeks or months. The storyteller, equipped with all types of stories—picture books, simple folktales, a short literary tale to read aloud—can help ease the child's concerns and bring the gift of shared pleasure. The storyteller on a visit to a hospital should be prepared to read to a group of children or to an individual child. Most likely the group will include a wide age range. A new storyteller went prepared to share picture books with young children. Her audience turned out to be a group of fifth- and sixth-grade boys. Fortunately, she knew a story that pleased them. Then she confessed her predicament and invited them to share her own delight in picture-book art. Because she had not talked down to them, the boys thoroughly enjoyed their introduction to the picture-book world.

There is a special need for reading aloud and storytelling in the clinic waiting room. Often parents must sit with their children a long time, waiting to be called by the doctor. The children become restless; they run and romp and very often are overexcited by the time the doctor is ready to examine them. Experience has shown that the medical staff usually welcomes a "quiet hour" before clinic time.

## Storytelling Outdoors

In many communities storytellers from the public library visit parks and playgrounds on a regular schedule of story hours, especially during the summer months. The summer storytelling program, which brings librarians into contact with readers and nonreaders, is often a child's introduction to the public library and to books. Storytellers on the staff of recreational centers and camps use the outdoors as the setting for the story hour. Informal storytelling is carried on while the children are resting after games or are just sitting around talking. However, during the scheduled period set aside for storytelling, the story is the primary activity. Many playgrounds have special story hours scheduled during the mornings when activity is slow. This keeps the group fairly small and easier to control.

Summer story hours in parks present a real challenge to storytellers. Often the groups are very large and have a broad age span—from toddlers to grandparents. Mothers bring their children, a recreation leader planning a picnic in the park sees the story-hour group and brings a group to join it (sometimes in the middle of the story), teenagers stop to listen, dogs bark and romp around in the periphery. Every possible distraction can be present. Such situations demand poise, a strong voice, and a careful selection of stories. The storyteller must be flexible and unflappable.

Find a quiet, shady secluded area, away from swimming, and wading pools and noisy play areas. Invite the children to sit on the ground in a semicircle with the smaller children in front. Give the children plenty of legroom. The storyteller usually stands so that the children can hear the story and see the storyteller more easily.

Plan the program for about 20 to 30 minutes. Bring along a few picture books with large, colorful pictures in case you need to begin your program with stories for the youngest. Tell two or three short surefire stories, full of dramatic action and a good helping of humor. Folktales are a wise choice. Keep the program relaxed and informal.

Storytelling is used extensively in camp programs. There is no set time to tell stories, but storytelling around a camp fire at night has a magic of its own. Use the locale, whether woods, seashore, or mountains. A starry night is the perfect time to tell legends of the stars and sky beings. Ghost stories are a favorite, but these are best reserved for telling to older boys and girls. Younger children enjoy scary stories in more familiar surroundings. On a rainy evening the leader might suggest that the youngsters take turns telling stories indoors. These round robins encourage children to become storytellers.

## Family Story Hours

This type of program is usually planned for early evening, about 7:30 or 8:00 P.M., so that the family has time to complete dinner and arrive at the story hour without feeling pressured and rushed. The early hour also allows time for a few minutes of visiting, browsing, and selecting books to take home, because this audience often leaves immediately after the program.

The family story hour is planned for older children—fourth graders and beyond—and their parents. Younger children must be brought at times, but whenever possible, parents should be encouraged to leave them at home with a babysitter. Older children need this occasional family excursion where they are the important members of the group rather than their younger brothers and sisters. It must be recognized, however, that some families find it difficult to leave the younger children at home, and so the storyteller should be prepared to adjust to some "younger child" distractions. If there are quite a few younger children in the audience and if a second staff member can be assigned to the program, this person can take the younger children aside and have a picture-book hour. Another possibility is to have volunteers—high school students or other parents—who will read to the younger children.

About 40 minutes should be allocated for the actual storytelling. Stories, poetry, and music suitable for the older group should be presented. Two stories with some poetry or music or three short stories allow flexibility for creative planning. A mixture of types is advisable—literary and folk, serious and humorous, quiet and active are all to be considered. Choose stories that can be appreciated on both a child and an adult level. Spencer Shaw, the well-known storyteller, held groups spellbound with his telling of "A Lover of Beauty," the story of Pygmalion and Galatea, from *Greek Myths*, by Olivia Coolidge (Houghton), when he conducted his Family Evening Story Hours in the Nassau County (New York) libraries. In speaking of the values of these story hours, Shaw said, "Parents experience a new relationship with their children: an emotional bond which finds release in shared laughter, shared adventure, shared confidences. Children experience a new understanding of their parents' concerns. Together, they enjoy a storyteller's art."[3]

In "Storytelling Programs for the Family," Carol Birch shares the obstacles and solutions she experienced when conducting the Family Storytelling Hour with Carol at the Craft and Folk Art Museum in Los Angeles, a program she conducted monthly for two years. The pattern Carol established was (1) a ritualistic, opening story, (2) a specific sharing time, (3) a story with broad appeal, (4) a more difficult story, (5) a participation story, and (6) a short scary or funny story to close. Carol had families sit together during the story hour, rather than the usual "children in front, adults in the back." This arrangement encouraged family members to touch and interact and to share the experience together.[4]

## Storytelling to Infants and Toddlers

Storytelling to children under age 3 was neglected until fairly recently. Library storytelling programs for preschoolers were designed for the 4- and 5-year-olds who were ready to participate in a group activity without the presence of parents/caregivers. As the theories of Jean Piaget became better known through translations of his writings, and as professionals became aware of the research of Burton White and others that demonstrated the importance of these early years in language development and interest in books and reading, library programs followed.

As early as the 1930s, libraries encouraged literature-sharing activities between mothers and infants through the Mothers' Rooms programs started by Charles Sumner, director of the Youngstown (Ohio) Public Library. However, with the advent of the Second World War and the exodus of women from the home to work in industry while men were at battle, these programs faded. After the war, women were encouraged to return to the home and have larger families, but librarians planning literature-sharing programs focused on children aged 3 to 5. The library preschool hour was considered the child's first introduction to stories in a group setting on his or her own. Parents/caregivers were discouraged from attending these programs.

But about the mid-1970s, storytimes for children under age 3 came into being. The new research emphasized the importance of the parent as the child's first teacher, and the new storytelling programs are parent/child programs. Parents/caregivers are present throughout the program and are encouraged to be active participants. (Figure 9.)

In a survey of library literature-sharing programs, Dr. Ann D. Carlson found a close correspondence between the type of activities offered and the developmental needs of young children.[5] These activities consist of the presentation of simple picture books, finger plays, songs, poems, and Mother Goose and nursery rhymes. The young child's introduction to literature is through the ear, so it seems appropriate for the program to include musical recordings or simple songs. Infants enjoy stories with interesting sound patterns and a lilting cadence. *The Baby's Lap Book*, by Kay Chorao (Dutton), and *The Random House Book of Mother Goose*, illustrated by Arnold Lobel (Random), are two examples of books infants enjoy. Toddlers are ready for more story. Try *The Elephant and the Bad Baby*, by Elfrida Vipont (Coward), *Mr. Gumpy's Motor Car*, by John Burningham (Harper), and the "I Can Do It All by Myself" series, by Shigeo Watanabe (Philomel).

Many librarians include a segment in which each infant or toddler chooses a book from a large basket of preselected books and takes it to the parent/caregiver to read aloud. The programs are limited to 15 or 20 minutes, but are long enough to give parents/caregivers an opportunity to discover the wide range of books available for the very young and to learn techniques of sharing literature with them. The children and their parents/caregivers find the experience mutually rewarding. Librarians interested in offering this type of program will find *Babies Need Books*, by Dorothy Butler (Atheneum), *Family Storybook Reading*, by Denny Taylor and Dorothy S. Strickland (Heinemann), and articles by Christopher Baar-Lindsay and Nancy Kewish,[6, 7] helpful resources.

FIGURE 9. Infant Story Hour at Wolfsohn Library, King of Prussia, Pennsylvania. (Photograph © Barbara Kernaghan.)

## Storytelling to Young Adults

Young adults often question storytelling as being an appropriate activity for them, but many of the values of storytelling discussed in Chapter 2 are pertinent to the needs of adolescents. The selection of the story and the storyteller's manner of presentation are of paramount importance.

This age audience is ready for stories that require some understanding of life's experience. "The Woodcutter of Gura," from Harold Courlander's *Fire on the Mountain* (Holt), is a good example of a subtle story that is lost on younger children. Many of the Appalachian mountain stories from *Grandfather Tales*, by Richard Chase (Houghton), and the Native American stories collected by John Bierhorst are excellent choices. Literary fairy tales are especially meaningful to young people at the time when they are becoming aware of their individuality and often find their values in conflict with society. They give the young adolescent courage to explore his or her inner space, dreams, images, feelings, and, through imagination, to construct a self. Adolescents can appreciate the underlying meaning, the humanistic philosophy, and the bittersweet mood so characteristic of the literary fairy tale. They are ready for the stories of Natalie Babbitt, Laurence Housman, Isaac Bashevis Singer, Oscar Wilde, and Jane Yolen. Housman, the humanist, strikes out against vanity, greed, and thoughtless cruelty in "Gammelyn, the Dressmaker" in *The Rat-Catcher's Daughter* (Atheneum). Babbitt pokes fun at our culture's emphasis on physical beauty as a requisite for happiness in "The Very Pretty Lady" in *The Devil's Storybook* (Farrar). Science fiction tales, ghost stories such as "Mary Culhane and the Dead Man" in *The Goblins Giggle, and Other Stories*, by Molly Bang (Scribner), and *Scary Stories to Tell in the Dark*, by Alvin Schwartz (Lippincott), are popular with young adults. The humor of James Thurber's *Fables for Our Time* and Anne Sexton's parodies of traditional fairy tales also appeal.

Storyteller Beth Horner recommends "a gradual exposure to storytelling by integrating it into successful existing programs or into situations in which the YA is a captive audience, such as the school assembly or classroom."[8] A guest storyteller can ask to be introduced as one who has come to talk about stories rather than as a storyteller. Sometimes talking briefly about storytelling as an ancient art originally told to an adult audience and the current revival of interest, with mention of the annual storytelling festival sponsored by the National Association for the Preservation and Perpetuation of Storytelling (NAPPS), indicates to your audience that this art is "not for children only." Or simply begin with your story. However, instead of beginning with the traditional "Once upon a time . . . ," consider "There was once. . . ." Tell your story in a straightforward manner, avoiding exaggerated voice changes or an overly dramatic style. Show your enjoyment of the story and your respect for both the story and the listeners' experience and intelligence.

Classroom projects, such as collecting family stories, using stories as a springboard to creative writing, or learning to tell stories to younger children (see Chapter 7), create an interest in storytelling for its own sake.

## Storytelling on Radio and Television

> To sustain a story on the air for twenty minutes or more with the use of only one instrument, the voice, although it may sound easy, is really a most demanding act. The storyteller's voice must have great range and flexibility. . . . He must convey the "feel" of each new character at once solely by the use of his voice.[9]

If you are invited to tell stories on radio and television, choose stories for their broad appeal, literary quality, action, and a minimum of detail. Folktales are excellent choices, though modern stories and literary fairy tales can be used. They should appeal to as wide an audience as possible. Select a story that requires no cutting or a minimum of cutting to fit the time allotted.

A 15-minute radio show is a good length; television producers usually want a 30-minute show. The latter must be planned with visuals, and so the story should be selected with this in mind. A story that requires 30 minutes to tell cannot be squeezed into a 15-minute time slot. Even shortening a story by 2 minutes requires substantial cutting, so try to find an appropriate story that is short enough to require very little change. Nevertheless, it is important to learn how to cut a story, if necessary. Do not eliminate all description, because this kind of background information is necessary in order to create a mood and establish atmosphere and visualization. A word here and there, an unnecessary phrase, a digression can all be eliminated. For example, cut "Once upon a time there was" to "Once there was." Eliminate adjectives where they seem superfluous. The result will be a tightened story, which becomes a script to be read word for word.

If the story you have chosen is not long enough for the allotted time, stretch the program with poetry or song or both. A lively theme song can be used as an introduction and a fade-out to set the mood for the program.

Plan programs well in advance. Obtain the permission of the publisher to use any copyrighted materials that are needed for the program. Be sure to give credit to the author, illustrator, and publisher of any book used, whether or not it is in copyright.

During the broadcast it is very important for the storyteller to watch the director or floor manager for cues and to follow directions. Be prepared to improvise, especially during the last few minutes of the program. Do not speak too quickly, but do not drag out the story. Enunciate clearly, use a natural manner and voice, avoid overdramatization, but do not eliminate all the drama in your telling, especially on radio. Use the dramatic pause and perfect its timing. Have a glass of water handy for that unexpected tickle in the throat. (The glass of water and any notes you have can be hidden from the camera by placing them behind your books.) Look directly into the camera, not at the monitor, and remember that the microphone picks up the slightest noise—a cleared throat, a sigh, the rattle of papers. It is difficult for most storytellers to tell a story to a microphone or to a camera, so try to picture a group of listeners in your mind as you tell. Let the enjoyment of the story come through in your voice if the medium is radio, and through your voice and facial expression if the medium is television.

## Notes

1. Craig Werner, "A Blind Child's View of Children's Literature," *Children's Literature* 12 (1984): 209–216.
2. Jed P. Luchow, "Selecting Picture Storybooks for Young Children with Learning Disabilities," in *Jump over the Moon*, by Pamela Petrick Barron and Jennifer Q. Burley (New York: Holt, 1984), p. 406.

3. Spencer G. Shaw, "A Story Falls in the Silence," *Wilson Library Bulletin*, October 1964, p. 179.
4. Carol Birch, "Storytelling Programs for the Family," *National Storytelling Journal*, Summer 1984, pp. 14–18.
5. Ann D. Carlson, *Early Childhood Literature Sharing Programs in Libraries* (Hamden, Conn.: Shoe String, 1985).
6. Christopher Baar-Lindsay, "Library Programming for Toddlers," *Public Libraries*, Fall 1983, pp. 111–113.
7. Nancy Kewish, "South Euclid's Pilot Project for Two-Year-Olds and Parents," *School Library Journal*, March 1979, pp. 93–98.
8. Beth Horner, "To Tell or Not to Tell: Storytelling for Young Adults," *Illinois Libraries*, September 1983, pp. 458–464.
9. Lilian Okun, *Let's Listen to a Story* (New York: Wilson, 1959), pp. 11–12.

## Titles Referred to in This Chapter

American Library Association. ALSC Library Service to Children with Special Needs Committee. *Programming for Children with Special Needs*. Chicago: American Library Association, 1981.

Babbitt, Natalie. *The Devil's Storybook*. New York: Farrar, 1974.

Bang, Molly. *The Goblins Giggle, and Other Stories*. New York: Scribner, 1973, o.p.

Baskin, Barbara Holland, and Harris, Karen H. *The Special Child in the Library*. Chicago: American Library Association, 1976.

Burningham, John. *Mr. Gumpy's Motor Car*. New York: Harper, 1976.

———. *Mr. Gumpy's Outing*. New York: Holt, 1971.

Burton, Virginia Lee. *Mike Mulligan and His Steam Shovel*. Boston: Houghton, 1939.

Butler, Dorothy. *Babies Need Books*. New York: Atheneum, 1982.

———. *Cushla and Her Books*. Boston: Horn Book, 1980.

Carle, Eric. *The Very Hungry Caterpillar*. New York: Philomel, 1981.

Carlson, Bernice Wells. *Listen and Help Tell the Story*. Nashville: Abingdon, 1965.

Chase, Richard. *Grandfather Tales*. Boston: Houghton, 1948.

Chorao, Kay. *The Baby's Lap Book*. New York: Dutton, 1977.

Coolidge, Olivia. *Greek Myths*. New York: Houghton, 1949.

Courlander, Harold. *The Fire on the Mountain and Other Ethiopian Stories*. New York: Holt, 1950, o.p.

Grimm, Jakob, and Grimm, Wilhelm. *The Shoemaker and the Elves*. Illustrated by Adrienne Adams. New York: Scribner, 1960.

Housman, Laurence. *The Rat-Catcher's Daughter*. New York: Atheneum, 1977, o.p.

Keats, Ezra Jack. *Whistle for Willie*. New York: Viking, 1964.

Lobel, Arnold. *The Random House Book of Mother Goose*. New York: Random, 1986.

Munari, Bruno. *The Birthday Present*. New York: World, 1959, o.p.

Schwartz, Alvin. *Scary Stories to Tell in the Dark*. New York: Lippincott, 1981.

Sendak, Maurice. *Where the Wild Things Are.* New York: Harper, 1963.

Sexton, Anne. *Transformations.* Boston: Houghton, 1971.

Taylor, Denny, and Strickland, Dorothy S. *Family Storybook Reading.* Portsmouth, N.H.: Heinemann, 1986.

Thurber, James. *Fables for Our Time.* New York: Harper, 1983.

Vipont, Elfrida. *The Elephant and the Bad Baby.* Illustrated by Raymond Briggs. New York: Coward, 1986.

Watanabe, Shigeo. "I Can Do It All by Myself" series. New York: Philomel, various dates.

# 7 Children and Young Adults as Storytellers

Children in the middle and upper grades enjoy telling stories to younger children, and younger children respond enthusiastically. The 10-year-old who shuns the library story hour as a program "for babies" may rediscover the power of stories as he or she relates them to peers or younger listeners.

The child as teller may seem a contemporary idea but in fact it was practiced in early library work with children. For instance, in 1917, the New York Public Library had 46 reading clubs with a membership of nearly 1,000 boys and girls. That year a special meeting was held to welcome Marie Shedlock to Staten Island. Each club sent a representative to the meeting. One young representative made this tribute to Marie Shedlock:

> Three or four years ago we were content to read stories and plays, but during the past two winters we have tried to tell stories ourselves and thus, Miss Shedlock, our ambition has been aroused to further your great work in reviving the art of storytelling.[1]

Across the country creative librarians and teachers are introducing children to the art of storytelling and reading aloud. Since 1969, Robert Rubinstein, a language arts teacher at Roosevelt Junior High/Middle School in Eugene, Oregon, has taught a class called "The Troupe of Tellers." The troupe consists of 12 sixth, seventh, and eighth grade students who tell stories and perform story-theater in classrooms, public libraries, camps, hospitals, and rest homes. In 1973, they received a "Great Kids" Award for public service from the state of Oregon.[2] Isabel Wilner, librarian of the laboratory school at Towson State College, began a Poetry Troupe, a group of elementary school children who go into the campus classrooms to read aloud to the college students. *The Poetry Troupe: An Anthology of Poems to Read Aloud*, compiled by Isabel Wilner (Scribner), is a collection of the children's favorite poems.

In this chapter we describe in detail three contemporary programs that may serve as models for adults who wish to introduce young people to the storyteller's art.

## "Reach for a Story" Project

Ocean County (New Jersey) Library's "Reach for a Story" project was designed for boys and girls in the fourth to sixth grades. The goals set by the coordinator of Children's Services, Emily Holman, and the storytelling consultant, Ellin Greene, were

1. To introduce children to the art of storytelling for their own enjoyment and for the entertainment of others.
2. To motivate children to read and to use the resources of the library.
3. To nurture the child's creative imagination.
4. To increase the child's communication skills—listening, speaking, reading, and writing.
5. To introduce children to folk literature and modern imaginative stories.
6. To guide children in the selection of tellable tales.
7. To teach children the techniques of learning and telling stories.
8. To build appreciation of cultural differences and similarities.
9. To encourage parents, teachers, librarians, and other professionals to use storytelling in their work with children.
10. To increase the visibility of the library and its program for children.

It was decided that each of the seven regions in the county system would hold a Mini-Festival, rather than a "contest," at which time *all* the children participating in the project would tell a story. The regional librarians, the storytelling consultant, the coordinator of children's services, and the young tellers would then select a representative from each region to tell at a Grand Festival to be held at the Main Library during Children's Book Week. The selections were made on the basis of the requirements for a good program (variety in theme, length of stories, and styles of telling) as well as on the proficiency of the teller. Every child who participated in the project received a certificate of recognition and a copy of the consultant's story anthology, *Midsummer Magic* (Lothrop). In addition, the seven representatives at the Grand Festival were presented with a book bag imprinted with a specially designed logo, "Reach for a Story," and a copy of Virginia Haviland's *Favorite Fairy Tales Told around the World* (Little), to encourage continuation of their newly learned craft. Three of the seven tellers later appeared on local cable television to talk about their experience in learning to be a storyteller and each told a story. Many of the children also told stories to classes in their schools.

The storytelling consultant presented two workshops for the children. In between the workshops the regional librarians met with the young tellers.

At the first workshop the storytelling consultant shared with the children a bit of historical background about storytelling gleaned from Ruth Sawyer's *The Way of the Storyteller* (Viking), Anne Pellowski's *The World of Storytelling* (Bowker), and notes accumulated over many years of reading and teaching. Facts, such as that the storyteller in medieval times enjoyed a high rank in society and sat near the king in the great hall or rode beside him in battle, that the storyteller was allowed to wear only one less color than the king (while ordinary folk were limited to one, two, or three colors), that there was a special storyteller's cloak made of bird feathers, that if captured in battle the storyteller's ransom was the high sum of 126 head of cattle, stirred the children's imagination.

After asking the children why they thought people told stories and where they thought stories came from, the consultant told them *A Story, a Story* (Atheneum), using the text of Gail Haley's picture book without the pictures. The consultant and the children talked about the pictures people see in their mind's eye as they listen to a story and they shared some of their pictures before looking at Ms. Haley's illustrations. It is always surprising to hear the many different pictures the same words evoke.

Next the consultant told a variant of a familiar folktale, such as "Cinderella" or "Rumpelstiltskin." Time permitting, the children were encouraged to become "folklorist-detectives," a term coined by Professor Jane Bingham of Oakland University. In this activity the children find other versions of the same tale or compare several picture-book editions of the same story. Thus the children learn that storytelling is a way of seeing. To help the children visualize the happenings in a story, the consultant told "Hafiz, the Stonecutter," from Marie Shedlock's *The Art of the Story-Teller* (Dover) and asked the children to list the happenings in the story in their proper order. Then the children made storyboards by drawing pictures of these happenings. (Figure 10.) The Shedlock version was chosen over the more familiar picture-book version by Gerald McDermott (Viking), primarily because it is not illustrated, thus encouraging the children to make their own images, but also because the Shedlock version has an upbeat ending and a message that struck a sympathetic chord with the young tellers—"Be Yourself." Before the children made their storyboards the children and the consultant discussed the story's circular pattern and the repetition of important phrases. The children were becoming aware of story form and the necessity of events occurring in logical sequence.

The storytelling consultant and the children talked about the many different kinds of stories—folktales, literary fairy tales, myths and legends, hero tales, tall tales, humorous stories, jokes, and ghost stories—and the qualities that make a story tellable (see pages 29–30). The children browsed in collections of tellable tales pulled from the folktale shelves before the workshop began. Individual consultations concluded the workshop.

Some children immediately found a story to work with, others took home one or two story collections to read before the next workshop. To find a story they would enjoy telling required browsing through several collections and reading many stories, one of the goals of the project. A few children found stories in places not anticipated by the staff. For instance, one girl chose a story about Detective Mole from Robert Quackenbush's easy-to-read mysteries (Lothrop). Another chose a short humorous tale, "What Hershel's Father Did," from *Cricket Magazine*.

The storyboard was presented as a memory jogger. Another memory aid used was the cue card. (Figure 3.) The children were encouraged to make a storyboard and a cue card for their story (cue card forms were provided). These were discussed the following week when the children met with their librarians. The librarians listened to the children's first attempts at storytelling and

FIGURE 10. Storyboard by Colleen Dolcy, Ocean County Library, New Jersey. Used by permission.

when necessary, assisted a child in finding a different story if the original choice wasn't working out.

At the second workshop the children worked on expression, language, and the use of kinesics in storytelling. They practiced phrasing, or what Kathryn Farnsworth[3] calls "where to take a breath," by marking up a story to indicate the shortest possible phrases. They said tongue twisters and "acted out" their stories. Bob Barton, in his *Tell Me Another* (Pembroke), recommends the use of call and response stories, chanting word play, drama games, and the like. Such approaches offer fun as well as opportunities for practice. The children enjoyed relaxation and voice exercises—jumping jacks, head and shoulder rolls, yawning, "ugly exercises" (see page 52), and imagining themselves as puppets (see page 51).

The children and the consultant talked about the importance of the beginning and ending of a story. With everyone speaking at the same time, to avoid self-consciousness, they said the first and last lines of their stories to suggest different states of emotion—surprise, boredom, sadness, anger, anxiety, pleasure. Then they listened to each other say the lines as the teller thought they should be said.

The teller identified the most important moment in the story and pantomimed the emotion of that moment, with the group guessing the emotion. They talked about effective—and noneffective—use of gestures, facial expressions, body movements. (Figure 11.)

Finally, the group gave a critique of the tellings. By asking, "What did you like about the way (storyteller's name) told the story?" and "Can you suggest anything (storyteller's name) might do to make the telling even better?" the consultant kept the group's criticism positive. Negative criticism, if any, should be offered by the group leader in private—and gently. Children, like adults, learn through experience.

The librarians met with the children a week later to hold a rehearsal for the Mini-Festivals. As often as possible the rehearsal took place in the same room as the Mini-Festival. In this way the children became familiar with the size and seating arrangement of the room and could practice projecting their voices in the more formal setting. They asked themselves: "Can the person sitting in

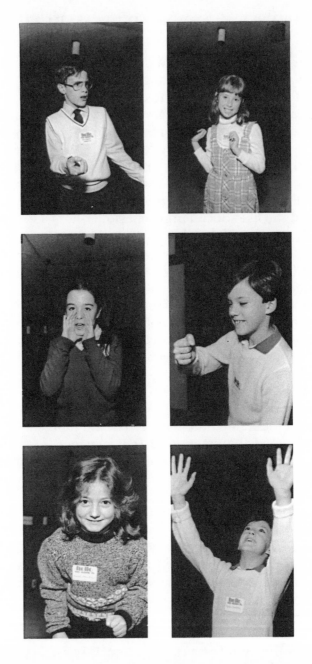

FIGURE 11. Tale-tellers of Ocean County (N.J.): Christopher Anderson (top left), Christina Estlow (top right), Lurana Brown (middle left), Dylan Cadalzo (middle right and bottom right), and Aimee Amodio (bottom left). (Photographs © John van Campenhout.)

the last row hear my story? Did I tell my story slowly enough so that the listeners had time to see the happenings in the story?" In several schools the librarian or media specialist arranged for the children to tell their stories during a class visit to the library. These experiences helped to polish the tellings. The regional librarians were astonished at the progress the young tellers made in such a short period of time, and at their poise and pleasure in telling before a group. Incidentally, the girls outnumbered the boys two to one, but the boys told with vigor and obviously enjoyed the experience. Parents noted an increase in self-confidence and in reading for pleasure. The children learned courtesy and how to be good listeners as well as good tellers.

Were there negative features? A few. Despite early resolutions to discourage competitiveness, a few teachers and librarians still conceived of the festivals as "contests." The authors agree with educator Bryon Padgett that "competitiveness that makes most kids feel anxious, unloved, and defeated, or vainly victorious" has no place in storytelling.[4]

The biggest problem was the uneven size of the groups in the regions. Some groups had as few as 4 children while others had as many as 22. The ideal size is 10 to 12 tellers. But public transportation is almost nonexistent in Ocean County and redistribution would have created a hardship. The regional librarian and the consultant each worked with half of the larger groups during the workshop tellings and critiques. The rewards far outnumbered the "problems."

## Storytelling Residencies in Schools

Many state arts councils sponsor "Artists-in-Education" programs. In recent years storytellers have become eligible to participate. The "Storyteller-in-Residence" arranges with the school principal and the teachers involved to meet with a specified number of classes over a specified number of weeks. Fourth and fifth graders are an especially responsive group to work with. The program requires a strong literature collection. The basic approach is similar to the one used in "Reach for a Story." However, school administrators often request some tie-in with the school curriculum. For instance, the children might study the folktales of a particular country or geographical region, or stories from different regions of the United States to fit in with a social studies program. Children can learn research skills and how to use the library's resources as they select, research, and learn a tale. Hearing a story, then having the children write the images remembered most, is a technique used by Storyteller-in-Residence Susan Danoff to demonstrate that we all choose different moments in a story, and even if we choose the same moment we see it differently—a natural lead-in to creative writing in the language arts curriculum. Beth Horner, another Storyteller-in-Residence, worked with a learning disabilities class to develop skills of verbal expression through telling stories that the children collected from members of their family.

Support from the faculty and agreement on possible residency activities (for example, workshops and classes for teachers, workshops and classes for students, consultation to teachers, performances and festivals) are essential for success. Scheduling can be complicated and working it out is time-consuming. The program usually runs over a period of six to eight weeks. During that time weekly lunchtime teacher workshops have been found to generate support. At the workshops one storytelling technique is discussed each week and exercises given for the teachers to try out with the students. The teachers are encouraged to read aloud or tell stories to the children *every day.* If it is not possible to hold short weekly workshops, hold a longer (60-to-90-minute) workshop at the beginning of the residency. This workshop should cover the values of storytelling, resources for the storyteller, techniques of learning and telling, what to expect of the young tellers, and a demonstration of storytelling.

The children first tell in their classrooms, then to younger children or peers in their schools. Schools may sponsor a festival night for parents and teachers featuring the young tellers. Storytellers who have worked in inner-city schools have noticed that the children develop a more positive self-image and increase their skills in communicating their thoughts and feelings. A fifth grader in one of Susan Danoff's storytelling residencies wrote,

> During these past few months in the storytelling group I have learned that anything that you put your mind to you can do. I real-

ized that with the help of Ms. Danoff and the other members of the storytelling group. Before I used to think I was hopeless in telling stories. But with encouragement from Ms. Danoff and the rest of the group not laughing every time I made a mistake, I made a remarkable achievement. Now my mother is proud of me, my teacher is proud of me, and most of all, I'm proud of myself.[5]

## Free Library of Philadelphia's Reading-Aloud Project

Reading aloud is often an avenue to storytelling and it is a way of introducing young people to the art. The Free Library of Philadelphia's Reading-Aloud Project is a model program.

When the program started in 1985, letters of invitation were mailed to potential participants identified by the staff and by public school librarians to participate in a series of four workshops in the art of reading aloud. The participants were mostly seventh and eighth graders, with some ninth and tenth graders. At the training sessions the staff demonstrated reading aloud, talked about the story's appeal or purpose, the intended audience, and the teller's feeling about the story. Reading aloud techniques were compared and contrasted with storytelling techniques. Different kinds of picture books were introduced. The participants selected books to take home to practice reading aloud.

The next week, the young people either read aloud to the entire group or were divided into small groups whose members took turns reading to each other. The second and third sessions included discussion of the use of finger plays, songs, audiovisual materials, etc. The young people were instructed in program planning, how to establish a listening atmosphere, and how to maintain order. The final session included reading aloud to the entire group and the presentation of certificates.

The Mayor's Commission on Literacy arranged for the presentation of a $10 gift certificate for a local bookstore to all who successfully completed the course. The participants were later assigned to read aloud on Saturdays at the public library or in the schools, day camp programs, and the zoo. These young people felt they had learned a great deal that would benefit them personally and the children with whom they worked. The library plans to continue the project indefinitely.[6]

## Notes

1. Report in the files of the Office of Children's Services, New York Public Library.
2. Robert E. Rubinstein, "Much More Than Just a Tale!" *National Storytelling Journal* (Fall 1986): 16.
3. Kathryn Farnsworth, "Storytelling in the Classroom—Not an Impossible Dream," *Language Arts* 58 (February 1981): 165.
4. Bryon Padgett, "The Care and Feeding of a Child's Imagination," *Ms. Magazine*, May 1976, p. 61.
5. John Marshall, P. J. Hill School, Trenton, New Jersey. From the personal files of Susan Danoff.
6. Information provided by Mrs. Florence Packer, Assistant Coordinator, Office of Work with Children, The Free Library of Philadelphia.

## Titles Referred to in This Chapter

Barton, Bob. *Tell Me Another: Storytelling and Reading Aloud at Home, at School and in the Community.* Markham, Ont.: Pembroke, 1986.

Greene, Ellin. *Midsummer Magic: A Garland of Stories, Charms, and Recipes.* New York: Lothrop, 1977, o.p. (Available from the author.)

Haley, Gail. *A Story, a Story: An African Tale.* Illustrated by Gail Haley. New York: Atheneum, 1970.

Haviland, Virginia. *Favorite Fairy Tales Told around the World.* Boston: Little, 1985.

McDermott, Gerald. *The Stonecutter: A Japanese Folk Tale.* New York: Viking, 1975.

Pellowski, Anne. *The World of Storytelling.* New York: Bowker, 1977.

Quackenbush, Robert. *Detective Mole and the Secret Clues.* New York: Lothrop, 1977.

Sawyer, Ruth. *The Way of the Storyteller.* New York: Viking, 1962.

Shedlock, Marie. *The Art of the Story-Teller*, 3rd ed. New York: Dover, 1951.

Wilner, Isabel. *The Poetry Troupe: An Anthology of Poems to Read Aloud.* New York: Scribner, 1977.

# 8 Program Planning

Careful planning, flexibility, and creativity are required for a successful storytelling program.

Planning ahead allows the storyteller to select stories to learn and to arrange them in a program that is a satisfying whole. Know the number of programs you are going to give during the year and the types of programs, such as regular story hours, holiday and special celebrations, family story hours, and others.

In planning the story hour consider the ages and interests of the children, their cultural or racial heritage, their listening capacity, and the scheduled length of the program. Selecting stories for children of similar background is not difficult, but often story-hour groups are composed of children of varying ages and interests. Although the story hour may consist of a single story, one that includes a variety of types of stories will appeal to the greatest number of children and make for a more interesting program. It will also provide a change of pace. Now is the time to go back to the cue cards that you have made from your readings. You have the titles, types of stories, sources, and synopses at your fingertips. In building your repertoire you have chosen different types of stories, stories of varying lengths and moods, and stories of universal appeal.

The storyteller learns with experience to judge the mood of the children and to adjust the program accordingly. Sometimes the choice of stories, though planned in advance, must be changed at the last minute. The public librarian does not always know who will be at the story hour and, therefore, must be prepared to make changes.

Because it is more difficult to establish a listening mood for the imaginative literary fairy tale than for the robust action of the folktale, it is usually best to tell the folktale first if your program includes both types of stories.

If possible, schedule separate story hours for the younger

children (5-to-7-year-olds), the middle-age children (8-to-10-year-olds), and the older children (11 years and older).

If you must, of necessity, tell to a group of children of mixed ages, plan to tell a story for the younger children first. The older children will be receptive if you explain that the story was chosen especially for the younger children. Then tell your main story and end with a short humorous tale. Take care that the story chosen for the younger children is not so simple in concept that it causes the older children to feel that they are too old for the entire program. The story for the older children must meet their interests and yet not be so far above the heads of the younger ones that they get nothing out of it. It is also possible to explain at the beginning of the program that the first story is for the younger children and that they may leave, if they wish, after it is told.

Three stories seem to work very well. The first story should catch the children's fancy; the second story may ask for a more thoughtful response or be more moving emotionally; the third should be easily comprehended and satisfying.

The program could be centered around a theme, such as "courage," a country, an author, or a subject. Or it may simply consist of stories that are unrelated in theme and yet balanced by type and mood. Other programs may focus on the birthdays of folklorists and writers of modern imaginative literature with the telling of their stories and poems.

Occasionally a teacher may request a story on a curriculum-related subject. However, the storyteller must be free to select material for the story hour and not tell a story for didactic purposes. Although storytelling may be used legitimately to support and enhance the curriculum, the teacher should respect the librarian-storyteller's right to choose the story.

## How Long Should the Story Hour Be?

The phrase "story hour" is misleading, because the story hour usually lasts less than 60 minutes. The age of the children, their past experience in story listening, and the library's or center's schedule all influence the length of the program. It may be as short as 15 minutes or as long as 1 hour. The length of time should be stated to eliminate the "coming and going" that breaks the mood and as a courtesy to parents who are providing transportation to and from the story hour. Begin on time and end as close to the announced time as possible. Many parents do not want their children to be out after dark and so, during the winter months, the story hour may have to be shortened or held at an earlier time.

## SAMPLE STORY HOURS

### Story Hour for Infants and Toddlers

Selections from "Music for 1's and 2's: Songs and Games for Young Children," sung and played by Tom Glazer. CMS Records, 1972. (CMS 649). For example, "Clap Hands" might be used to introduce or close the program or for a change of pace between stories.
*Brown Bear, Brown Bear, What Do You See?*, by Bill Martin, Jr. (Holt)
*How Do I Put It On?*, by Shigeo Watanabe (Philomel)
*But Where Is the Green Parrot?*, by Thomas Zacharias (Delacorte)

### Story Hour for Children Ages 3 to 5

*What's in Fox's Sack?*, by Paul Galdone (Clarion)
"The Bed," in *The Tiger and the Rabbit and Other Tales*, by Pura Belpre (Lippincott)
*The Gunniwolf*, by Wilhelmina Harper (Dutton)

### Story Hours for Children Ages 6 to 8

"Alligator's Sunday Suit," in *Bo Rabbit Smart for True: Folktales from the Gullah*, retold by Priscilla Jaquith (Philomel)
*Godfather Cat and Mousie*, retold after the Brothers Grimm, by Doris Orgel (Macmillan), or the Haitian version, "Uncle Bouqui and Godfather Ti-Malice," in *Uncle Bouqui of Haiti*, by Harold Courlander (Morrow)
*Wiley and the Hairy-Man*, by Molly Garrett Bang (Macmillan)

### Story Hour for Children Ages 8 to 11

"The Wonderful Brocade," in *The Spring of Butterflies and Other Chinese Folk Tales*, by He Liyi (Lothrop). *The Enchanted Tapestry*, by Robert D. San Souci (Dial), and *The Weaving of a Dream*, by Marilee Heyer (Viking) are picture-book versions of the same story.
"Two of Everything," in *The Treasure of Li-Po*, by Alice Ritchie (Harcourt), o.p. Also in *The Magic Umbrella*, by Eileen Colwell (Bodley Head)

## Story Hour for a Mixed-Age Group

"Molly Whuppie," in *Tales Told Again*, by Walter de la Mare (Knopf). The picture-book version illustrated by Errol Le Cain (Farrar) is based on de la Mare's telling.
"Cap o'Rushes," in *English Fairy Tales*, by Joseph Jacobs (Dover)

## Caribbean Story Hour

*The Cat's Purr*, by Ashley Bryan (Atheneum)
"I'm Tipingee, She's Tipingee, We're Tipingee, Too" in *The Magic Orange Tree and Other Haitian Folktales*, by Diane Wolkstein (Knopf)
*Perez and Martina*, by Pura Belpre (Warne). (For storytellers who would like to learn this traditional Puerto Rican folktale in Spanish, listen to Pura Belpre's telling on CMS 505.)

## Story Hour for Young Adults

"White Bear Whittington," in *Grandfather Tales*, by Richard Chase (Houghton)
"Mr. Fox," in *English Fairy Tales*, by Joseph Jacobs (Dover)
"The Yellow Ribbon," in *The Rainbow Book of American Folk Tales and Legends*, by Maria Leach (World). Also in *Juba This and Juba That*, by Virginia Tashjian (Little)

## Family Story Hour

"The Woman Who Flummoxed the Fairies," in *Heather and Broom: Tales of the Scottish Highlands*, by Sorche Nic Leodhas (Holt)
"Uncle Bouqui Rents a Horse," in *Uncle Bouqui of Haiti*, by Harold Courlander (Morrow)
"The Mixed-Up Feet and the Silly Bridegroom," in *Zlateh the Goat and Other Stories*, by Isaac B. Singer (Harper)

## Story Hour in Honor of an Author

Speak briefly about the story's author, Eleanor Farjeon
Read from *Eleanor Farjeon's Poems for Children* (Lippincott)
Tell "Elsie Piddock Skips in Her Sleep," in *Martin Pippin in the Daisy Field*, by Eleanor Farjeon (Lippincott)

## The Multimedia Program

The multimedia program combines two or more art forms, each of which can stand on its own—storytelling, film, music, dance—into a creative whole. This type of program appeals to many storytellers, especially the librarian or media specialist who feels there is not enough time to learn a sufficient number of stories to sustain a regularly scheduled storytelling program. In truth, it takes as much time to plan and select materials for a multimedia program as it takes to learn more stories. However, some people prefer the varied activity involved in preparing this type of program, such as previewing films and listening to recordings, to selecting and learning a story. The cultural experience that this kind of program offers children justifies the choice.

Storytelling can combine very well with other art forms, provided that the program is carefully thought out and the various parts related. The most effective programs usually are those that center around a theme or person. A school library media specialist planned a multimedia program with a spring theme for kindergarten children. She read *When the Root Children Wake Up*, by Helen D. Fish (Lippincott), using the opaque projector to show the pictures on the center of three screens. On the side screens she showed slides of buds bursting and flowers in bloom as she played a recording of "The Waltz of the Flowers" from Tchaikovsky's *Nutcracker Suite*. Spontaneously, these young children went up to the screen to touch the flowers—they looked so real—and began to dance to the music. It was a beautiful experience for both the librarian and the children.

The preparation of this kind of program involves careful selection of materials. Start with a theme, subject, or person. Bibliographies, such as *A Multimedia Approach to Children's Literature: A Selected List of Films (and Videocassettes), Filmstrips, and Recordings Based on Children's Books*, edited by Mary Alice Hunt (ALA), *Films Kids Like*, by Susan Rice (ALA), *More Films Kids Like*, by Maureen Gaffney (ALA), and the indexes to fairy tales by Mary Eastman and by Norma Ireland (Faxon), will help you to locate materials.

For a multimedia program to be successful, there must be a flow, a rhythm. The parts should complement each other, but each segment should be strong enough to stand on its own. If you use a film, choose one that is artistic. But remember that the story is as important as the film, dance, or other art form used. Generally, it is best for the story to come before the film, unless the film helps to establish a listening mood for the story.

A recording can be used to set the mood, for a change of pace, or to hear an author's voice. Music usually is used to introduce or conclude the program and sometimes to enhance the narrated story, a technique that has been perfected by storyteller Spencer Shaw. The storyteller who is interested in using this technique should read Shaw's article "Recorded Magic for Story Hours" and should be prepared to spend many hours in practice. The music must be "integrated artistically. . . . [It] blends with the words and mood so that it never becomes a foreign, musical intrusion. The story is the thing. The music merely heightens the emotional impact in certain passages or makes specific word pictures more meaningful."[1]

Preparing a well-balanced program is not sufficient in the case of a multimedia story hour. The storyteller must also pay careful attention to the physical and mechanical requirements of the program. Check the condition of any films and recordings to be used.

Reserve any audiovisual equipment needed. Arrange for a competent projectionist if you need help. Be prepared for equipment failure.

Arrange for a room that can be darkened if you plan to show a film. Check electrical outlets. Allow time to set up the equipment before the program begins.

Arrange the seating so that you will be able to switch from one medium to another without having the children move.

Just before the program, check the audiovisual equipment again. Focus any film or filmstrip you plan to show.

Now relax, and enjoy the program with the children.

## SAMPLE MULTIMEDIA PROGRAMS

### Program in Honor of an Author

Speak briefly about Carl Sandburg
Play recording of Carl Sandburg reading "How to Tell Corn Fairies When You See 'Em" (Caedmon TC 1159)
Tell "The White Horse Girl and the Blue Wind Boy," in *Rootabaga Stories*, by Carl Sandburg (Harcourt)
Show the film "Dream of the Wild Horses" (Contemporary Films) 9 min., color, 1960

### Program in Celebration of Black History Month

Give a brief biography of James Weldon Johnson, based on the introduction in *God's Trombones*, by James Weldon Johnson. New York: Viking, 1927.

Show the film "The Creation" (Will Vinton) 9 min., color, 1981. Narrated by James Earl Jones.

Read "Go Down Death" from *God's Trombones*, by James Weldon Johnson. New York: Viking, 1927.

End program with audience singing "Lift Every Voice and Sing," words by James Weldon Johnson and music by J. Rosamond Johnson. (As audience assembles for the program, distribute mimeographed sheets of the words.)

## Program with a Midsummer Theme

Introductory music: Incidental music from "A Midsummer Night's Dream," by Felix Mendelssohn (Seraphim S-60056)

Talk about the folklore of Midsummer Festival

Tell a story from *Midsummer Magic: A Garland of Stories, Charms, and Recipes*, by Ellin Greene (Lothrop)

## Magic Program

Theme music: "Magical Mystery Tour," by the Beatles (Capitol SMAL-02835)

Show the film "People Soup" (Learning Corp.) 13 min., color, 1970

Tell "Don't Blame Me," in *The Wonder Dog: The Collected Children's Stories of Richard Hughes* (Morrow)

Magic tricks demonstration

# Note

1. Spencer Shaw, "Recorded Magic for Story Hours," *Top of the News* 15 (October 1958): 43–47.

# Titles Referred to in This Chapter

Abdul, Raoul. *The Magic of Black Poetry.* New York: Dodd, 1972.

Bang, Molly Garrett. *Wiley and the Hairy-Man.* New York: Macmillan, 1976.

Belpré, Pura. *Perez and Martina.* New York: Warne, 1961, o.p.

———. *The Tiger and the Rabbit and Other Tales.* New York: Warne, 1965, o.p.

Bryan, Ashley. *The Cat's Purr.* New York: Atheneum, 1985.

Chase, Richard. *Grandfather Tales.* New York: Houghton, 1948.

Colwell, Eileen. *The Magic Umbrella.* London: Bodley Head, 1976.

Courlander, Harold. *Uncle Bouqui of Haiti.* New York: Morrow, 1942, o.p.

De la Mare, Walter. *Molly Whuppie.* Illustrated by Errol Le Cain. New York: Farrar, 1983.

———. *Tales Told Again.* New York: Knopf, 1959; Winchester, Mass.: Faber, 1980.

Eastman, Mary. *Index to Fairy Tales, Myths, and Legends.* Boston: Faxon, 1926. Supplements 1 and 2. 1937, 1952. o.p.

Farjeon, Eleanor. *Eleanor Farjeon's Poems for Children.* Philadelphia: Lippincott, 1951, 1984.

————. *Martin Pippin in the Daisy Field.* Philadelphia: Lippincott, 1937, o.p.

Fish, Helen D. *When the Root Children Wake Up.* Philadelphia: Lippincott, 1941, o.p.

Gaffney, Maureen. *More Films Kids Like.* Chicago: American Library Association, 1977.

Galdone, Paul. *What's in Fox's Sack?* New York: Clarion, 1982.

Gerson, Mary-Jane. *Why the Sky Is Far Away: A Folktale from Nigeria.* New York: Harcourt, 1974, o.p.

Gleason, Judith. *Orisha: The Gods of Yorubaland.* New York: Atheneum, 1971, o.p.

Greene, Ellin. *Midsummer Magic: A Garland of Stories, Charms, and Recipes.* New York: Lothrop, 1977, o.p. (Available from the author.)

Harper, Wilhelmina. *The Gunniwolf.* New York: Dutton, 1967.

Hughes, Richard. *The Wonder Dog: The Collected Children's Stories of Richard Hughes.* New York: Morrow, 1977, o.p.

Hunt, Mary Alice, ed. *A Multimedia Approach to Children's Literature: A Selected List of Films (and Videocassettes), Filmstrips, and Recordings Based on Children's Books,* 3rd ed. Chicago: American Library Association, 1983.

Ireland, Norma. *Index to Fairy Tales: 1949–1972.* Boston: Faxon, 1973.

Jacobs, Joseph. *English Fairy Tales.* New York: Dover, 1898.

Jaquith, Priscilla. *Bo Rabbit Smart for True: Folktales from the Gullah.* New York: Putnam, 1981.

Johnson, James Weldon. *God's Trombones.* New York: Viking, 1927.

Johnson, James Weldon, and Johnson, J. Rosamond. *Lift Every Voice and Sing.* New York: Hawthorn, 1970.

Leach, Maria. *The Rainbow Book of American Folk Tales and Legends.* New York: World, 1958, o.p.

Liyi, He. *The Spring of Butterflies and Other Chinese Folk Tales.* New York: Lothrop, 1985.

Martin, Bill, Jr. *Brown Bear, Brown Bear, What Do You See?* New York: Holt, 1983.

Orgel, Doris. *Godfather Cat and Mousie.* New York: Macmillan, 1986.

Rice, Susan, ed. *Films Kids Like.* Chicago: American Library Association, 1973.

Ritchie, Alice. *The Treasure of Li-Po.* New York: Harcourt, 1949, o.p.

San Souci, Robert D. *The Enchanted Tapestry.* New York: Dial, 1987.

Sandburg, Carl. *Rootabaga Stories.* New York: Harcourt, 1951.

Serwadda, W. Moses. *Songs and Stories from Uganda.* New York: Crowell, 1974.

Tashjian, Virginia A. *Juba This and Juba That.* Boston: Little, 1969.

Watanabe, Shigeo. *How Do I Put It On?* New York: Philomel, 1977.

Wolkstein, Diane. *The Magic Orange Tree and Other Haitian Folktales.* New York: Knopf, 1978.

Zacharias, Thomas. *But Where Is the Green Parrot?* New York: Delacorte, 1978.

# 9 Administration: Planning and Publicity

Questions have been raised about the role of the story hour and its importance in a time of budget cuts and diminishing staff. Public librarians and school library media specialists may need to convince their administrators as well as other members of their staffs that the story hour is a basic part of library service to children.

## How Are Nonstorytellers Convinced of the Value of the Story Hour?

Unmeasurable intangibles, felt by the storyteller, are difficult to convey to others. Exposure to the art is one of the best ways to win over nonbelievers. Invite administrators, librarians serving adults, principals, and teachers to observe a story hour where they can see for themselves the response of the children.

Both public librarians and school library media specialists can reach parents at PTO meetings. Family story hours, held in the evening, will convince many parents of the value of the story hour, and they will support this program with both administrators and board members.

Plan a storytelling festival as a special event of the children's department and invite both staff and community.

Suggest to your administrator the possibility of presenting a storytelling program at a staff or faculty meeting.

Invite your administrator or principal to accompany you to a storytelling festival sponsored by the public library.

Seek invitations to tell stories to community groups of adults, and then describe your program. Be alert to the possibility of inclusion in community programs.

### Should the Art of Storytelling Be Included in the Administrator's In-Service Education Plans?

Administrators of public libraries, schools, and recreation centers recognize the need for the in-service education of their staffs, both professional and nonprofessional. Librarians, teachers, and recreational workers should insist that storytelling be one of the subjects covered in these sessions. Even graduates of library schools and colleges of education need this extra instruction, because it is not fully covered in most universities. The administrator of a public library with a storytelling specialist on the staff can offer this specialist's services to other organizations in the community. Likewise, school administrators can share the expertise of their school library media specialists with teachers, aides, and others interested in storytelling.

### Should Preparation Time Be Given during the Working Day for Selecting and Learning Stories?

Administrators often raise the question about the time needed to prepare for a story hour. Much depends on the storyteller's ability to learn and retain. Some storytellers will find this easy and quick, whereas others will need a great deal of time. Certainly time should be allotted to search for the stories, because the reading of many books adds to the librarian's expertise in guiding readers. This reading cultivates and deepens the critical ability of the storyteller, who then gains in the appreciation of literary values. Books are important tools of the librarian's profession, and, as such, some time should be given to their examination and use. Realistically, much of the preparation done by storytellers is on their own time, but so is that of other professionals.

### Should Part of the Budget of a Children's Librarian or Media Specialist Be Used for Noncirculating Books to Support the Storytelling Program?

Books from which the storyteller has selected stories or poems need to be available at all times for planning and learning. The absence of a storytelling collection means that the choice of stories will be governed by the books that are on the shelves. This usually means that the most popular books will not be available to the storyteller.

A strong collection of reference books about storytelling and its related subjects is necessary for the storyteller's background reading (see Appendix 2). Such basic collections as Asbjørnsen and Møe's *East of the Sun and West of the Moon*, edited and illustrated by Ingri and Edgar Parin d'Aulaire (Viking), *The Glass Slipper: Charles Perrault's Tales of Times Past*, translated by John Bierhorst (Four Winds), the Lucy Crane, Lore Segal, and Ralph Manheim translations of the collected tales of the Brothers Grimm, and the M. R. James and Erik Haugaard translations of Hans Christian Andersen stories are necessary for comparative judgments of other translations. Clean books are necessary for the story-hour table and for display. These extra copies are not luxuries. They are part of the storyteller's professional library and are as necessary as the administrator's books on school or public library administration. They may have to be referred to as "the storyteller's professional shelf" in order to justify the expenditure of the necessary money.

## PLANNING

### What Are Some of the Steps in Planning a Story-Hour Program?

The first step is to coordinate the story-hour schedule with that of the library, school, or recreation center. In scheduling programs, consider the availability of space and staff. The story hour should be part of the entire programming plan, and so the day of the week as well as the frequency of the program is often governed by the overall schedule of events. It is also necessary to be aware of events in the community so that there is not too much scheduled at the same time for the same audience. Each organization will select the best day and time for its users.

School and public libraries should coordinate their story-hour schedules. It is often necessary to experiment with the days until the best one evolves. A public library often schedules the story hour on the day when the most children are in the library. The time of day is usually 4:00 P.M. (after school hours) or an appropriate time on Saturday. This time also would be appropriate for recreation centers. The school library media center would schedule a story hour within the school day. It might be possible to have a story hour during lunchtime for those children who do not go home for lunch. Busing presents a problem for after-school activities, but there may be enough children who are not bused to have a media-center story hour after school hours. The classroom teacher can select a day and time for a scheduled story hour, a time when he or she is free from teaching. This will add much to the children's enjoyment of books and reading. The teacher also should be alert to every opportunity for informal, spur-of-the-moment storytelling.

## How Often Should Story Hours Be Held?

Many factors enter into the decision to have weekly, monthly, semimonthly, or occasional special story hours. A neighborhood with few organized activities for children might very well need more frequent story hours for the 6- to 10-year-olds than one with highly organized recreational and school activities and overscheduled children—those whose after-school hours are mostly taken up with dancing lessons, violin lessons, choir practice, scouts, and other activities. The number of available storytellers is an important factor because it is practically impossible for one storyteller to learn well two or three stories every week and, at the same time, carry out other library responsibilities. What should be an enjoyable experience becomes a chore, the quality of storytelling suffers, and attendance at story hours begins to drop because of the lack of careful planning and good preparation. A weekly story hour should be undertaken only when more than one storyteller is available.

Public libraries with more than one branch children's librarian can consider the feasibility of "swapping" storytellers. The easiest way to do this is to have all the story hours in the branches scheduled at the same time. Then the storytellers can plan together a schedule of rotation. The administration must agree to this schedule before it is made final, because different librarians will be covering each children's room during this period. The administrator may object to this plan if the children's librarian also is called upon to be in charge of the branch when the administrator is absent. In other words, the storyteller's schedule should fit into the administrator's schedule.

One of the benefits of the swapping plan is that each storyteller involved has an opportunity to tell the same stories more than once. Even though each storyteller is telling stories weekly, there is more time to prepare new stories. This schedule also brings "guest storytellers" to the children. The planner should ask that a "home" person be scheduled in the children's room, if possible, in order to familiarize the visiting storyteller with the physical aspects of the room as well as to introduce the visitor to the children. If this schedule is carried over for a reasonable length of time, the visitor ceases to be a visitor and is accepted as a "home staffer."

The school library media specialist can often find parents, teachers, and even older children (see Chapter 7) who can be trained in storytelling and so enable more story hours to be scheduled. One high school media specialist who enjoys telling stories is released periodically from her regular schedule to go into elementary schools in her midwestern community to share her love of storytelling with the younger children and their teachers.

### Why Is It Best to Plan in Advance?

The storyteller can be more creative in programming if plans are made in advance. There is time to select stories and other materials carefully and to learn the stories well enough to be comfortable with them. If one plans an entire storytelling program, perhaps from Halloween to May Day, the decision can be made, for example, also to celebrate Hans Christian Andersen's birthday (April 2), and the selection and preparation of the stories can begin in October.

### Should Adults Be Permitted to Attend the Story Hour?

If you are a stranger to the group, it can be helpful to have the group leader settle the children. Teachers who bring their classes to the library for story hour should stay to *listen*; they should not grade papers or perform other chores during storytelling. Lack of interest on the part of adults carries over to the children.

Occasionally, a visiting storyteller or a student observer will be in the group. Observing experienced storytellers is an important part of the training of beginners and should be permitted. If there are too many adults in the group, however, the mood may be changed. The presence of adults can be threatening to children and can suppress their spontaneous responses to the story. If adults are curious about what takes place in the story hour, it is better to videotape a story hour for them or to schedule a family story hour. The sensitive librarian or teacher will know when to make an exception. In a predominantly Spanish-speaking community in New York City, adults were allowed to sit at the back of the story-hour room. By permitting them to stay, the librarian was able to establish a rapport with parents recently arrived from Puerto Rico and to help them feel at home in the library. The parents in turn enriched the library by sharing their culture and strongly supporting the library's storytelling program.

## PUBLICITY

### What Is the Importance of a Community File?

The dissemination of publicity depends largely upon your knowledge of key people in the community and your ability to gain their interest and cooperation. An up-to-date file of community organizations and people, complete with addresses, phone numbers, and any other necessary information, is a necessity. Generally speaking, the response is best when directed to one person in the organization—the principal or school library media specialist, the director of the day-care center or recreation center, the president of the parents' organization, the minister of the church. Newspapers and television and radio stations also respond best when the publicity is sent to a specific person with whom you have communication. Fliers, posters, and letters should be sent to this person with a request for posting, distribution, and public announcements.

### Do Personal Relationships Enter into Good Publicity?

A personal visit with the key people in an organization is very important. This is an opportunity to describe the storytelling program and the philosophy behind it. Many people must be convinced of the importance of story hours before they will publicize them. Invite these adults to attend a story hour so that they will feel more knowledgeable and involved. However, do not encourage frequent attendance because adults in a children's story hour often inhibit both the storyteller and the children. Invite them to attend a family story hour or an outdoor story hour where all ages are involved. Building good personal relationships will gain support for your program and can save time, too, as it often makes it possible to ask for publicity for future story hours over the phone.

## What Are the Best Kinds of Publicity?

Storytellers soon learn what is the most effective publicity for both the adult community and the children. Fliers can be placed in such places as restaurants, barber shops, beauty salons, grocery stores, staff rooms of schools and recreation centers, churches, and other public places frequented by adults. Storytellers can distribute fliers to children so long as the children retain them and do not throw them on the street or contribute to litter. Each librarian, teacher, or recreation worker is the best judge of distribution to children. A well-designed poster, placed in a library, school, recreation center, or playground, is an attention getter.

Important facts must be presented in both posters and fliers. These should include such items as the ages for which the story hour is planned, the place and time of the program, where tickets, if used, and additional information are available. When specifying the time it is well to mention limits, such as 4:00 P.M. to 4:45 P.M. This enables children and parents to have some idea of the length of the program.

In designing the fliers and posters, make them as simple as possible, but eye-catching. In her article "Storytelling Programs for the Family,"[1] Carol Birch includes an example of an effective publicity poster and one that does not project a positive image of storytelling. (Figure 12.)

> Note the two posters created for the storyhour. The poster of the girls listening to a read story . . . [implies that] storytelling and reading are the same; stories attract (and are reserved for?) sweet,

FIGURE 12. Example of an effective publicity poster (bottom) and one that does not project a positive image of storytelling (top). From *The National Storytelling Journal*, Summer 1984, p. 17.

young, old-fashioned, white girls—not active children, not older children, not modern children, not other races, not even boys; stories are shared by bland, featureless girls/children/women who seem inconsequential at best.

The second poster with the image of Pegasus offers a much more positive representation of storytellers. The graphic was adapted from a photograph of a painting by Susan Hefernan, an artist in New York City, and communicates the promise and strength inherent in stories.

It suggests that: stories are strong; stories illuminate like the sun, creating sharp contrasts of darkness and light; stories are winged things like Pegasus himself. Stories take one to a precipice where rationalistic explanations fall away—a place to soar or fall; stories exist at the very edge of night and day—at the edge of unconscious and conscious mind. The graphic is bold and the image evocative, drawing on the rich legacy of myth.

There are books of designs and illustrations that are made to be traced or even cut out, such as *The Dover Pictorial Archives*, a collection of out-of-copyright illustrations published by Dover Publications. If an illustration from a copyrighted book is desired, it is necessary, of course, to get permission for its use from the publisher. Explore and use the artistic talents of your coworkers and friends. Invite the art class in a school to submit designs. The use of chalkwalk, sandwich boards, balloons, and other fun-type publicity is described in Caroline Bauer's *Handbook for Storytellers* (ALA).[2]

Another source of free publicity is the local radio station. Radio stations are usually willing to make spot announcements about community programs.

One-to-one publicizing is always effective, and children seem to remember this better than printed forms of publicity. Personal urging to attend the next story hour makes the child feel especially wanted. The same "over-the-desk" conversation with parents also is effective. Some storytellers use free tickets as a reminder of the story hour.

If there is a public relations officer on the staff of the library or recreation center, publicity probably will be handled by that person. It then becomes the responsibility of the storyteller to get the necessary information to the public relations officer as early as possible.

## What Is the Purpose of the Story-Hour Ticket?

Story-hour tickets—free, of course—are a means of publicizing the story hour and of controlling the size of the group. Some storytellers in public libraries issue a seasonal ticket to the story-hour program. The ticket is punched each time the child attends. Older children who are familiar with series tickets to concerts and theatrical performances like the idea of a seasonal story-hour ticket. Seasonal tickets are issued at the beginning of the season, which usually runs from October to May.

Tickets for individual story hours usually are distributed a day or two before the program or just before the story hour begins, at the place of the program. These tickets are collected as the children enter or leave the story-hour area.

## Notes

1. Carol L. Birch, "Storytelling Programs for the Family," *National Storytelling Journal*, Summer 1984, p. 17.
2. Caroline Feller Bauer, *Handbook for Storytellers* (Chicago: American Library Association, 1977), pp. 26–34.

## Titles Referred to in This Chapter

Andersen, Hans Christian. *The Complete Fairy Tales and Stories.* Translated from the Danish by Erik Christian Haugaard. New York: Doubleday, 1974.

———. *Favorite Tales of Hans Andersen.* Translated from the Danish by M. R. James. Winchester, Mass.: Faber, 1986.

Asbjørnsen, Peter Christen, and Møe, Jorgen. *East of the Sun and West of the Moon.* Illustrated by Ingri and Edgar Parin d'Aulaire. New York: Viking, 1969, o.p.

Bauer, Caroline. *Handbook for Storytellers.* Chicago: American Library Association, 1977.

Grimm, Jakob, and Grimm, Wilhelm. *Grimm's Tales for Young and Old: The Complete Stories.* Translated by Ralph Manheim. New York: Doubleday, 1983.

———. *Household Stories of the Brothers Grimm.* Translated from the German by Lucy Crane. New York: Dover, 1963.

———. *The Juniper Tree and Other Tales from Grimm.* Translated from the German by Lore Segal and Randall Jarrell. New York: Farrar, 1973.

Perrault, Charles. *The Glass Slipper: Charles Perrault's Tales from Times Past.* Translated by John Bierhorst. New York: Four Winds, 1981.

# Appendix 1

# In-Service Education

## Planning a Storytelling Workshop

Establish the objectives of the workshop. What do you want to happen to the participants as a result of attending the workshop?

Define the audience you want to reach. Are they librarians, teachers, recreational leaders, staff, volunteers?

Plan a budget. How much money is needed?

How much time is available—a half day, a full day, several half-day sessions, a weekend?

How many leaders are available? Will it be a one-leader workshop? One leader plus an inspirational keynote speaker? One leader and several resource persons?

Will the participants meet as one large group or will the group be divided into smaller interest groups?

What aspects of storytelling will be covered?

What kinds of presentation and involvement methods would be most effective in achieving the objectives?

One-and-a-half-hour or two-hour sessions are long enough to get into a topic and cover major points without tiring the audience. Keep the workshop groups reasonably small (10–25 persons). Larger groups can be accommodated, but the presentations will tend to be lectures. It is hard to have a good discussion in a large group and impossible for everyone to tell a story and receive feedback.

Any storytelling workshop should provide an opportunity for the participants to hear good storytelling. If possible, arrange for children to be present at one of the storytelling demonstrations so that beginning storytellers can see an experienced storyteller interacting with children and handling some of the typical situations that arise.

Design an attractive flier stating the time, place, program, and registration information. Mail the flier to the expected audience in ample time to complete registration at least two weeks before the date of the workshop. Publicize your workshop through direct mail, professional journals, local organizations, library systems, newspapers, and radio.

If you plan to sell any storytelling materials at the workshop, order the materials on consignment from the publishers or a jobber far in advance of the workshop date. Arrange for at least two persons to handle the sales table, and be sure to have cash, including change, on hand.

Allow enough time to order any audiovisual materials you plan to use, to gather together an exhibit of books, and to prepare a bibliography. If you plan to use a film, reserve the projector well in advance. Be sure to have a projectionist available so that the workshop leader does not have this responsibility. Set up the equipment, and adjust the focus and sound before the workshop begins.

Arrange for comfortable meeting rooms. If a meal is to be served, plan an attractive but light menu. Coffee, tea, or juice served during the registration period is always welcome.

Have an attractive exhibit of books and other storytelling materials prominently displayed in a comfortable area. The exhibit should extend the participants' knowledge of storytelling literature. Allow time for browsing.

The introduction by the workshop leader or keynote speaker sets the tone for the workshop. The atmosphere should be relaxed, friendly, supportive so that the participants will be more at ease when they tell a story or participate in discussion. The workshop leader should outline to participants what they will be doing and the time schedule.

From the beginning, plan some form of evaluation. Evaluation is concerned with how well the objectives were reached.

Any workshop, and especially one planned for 100 or more persons, takes a tremendous amount of planning and coordination with all departments involved, from maintenance staff to top administration. The hard work that goes into a workshop should not show on the day of the workshop. Take care of the nitty-gritty beforehand so that the workshop runs as smoothly as possible, but always be prepared for the unexpected.

An in-staff workshop for beginning storytellers can be held once a week over a period of four to five weeks. Each session should be approximately 2 hours long. The workshop leader should be an experienced storyteller.

Session 1   Purpose and values of storytelling.
            Selection of materials.
            Demonstration of storytelling.
            Bibliography of storytelling literature distributed.
            Participants asked to read widely from books listed on the
                bibliography and to select stories they want to learn.
Session 2   Selection of materials (continued).
            Discussion of stories selected by the participants.

Preparation and presentation—techniques of learning and telling stories.

Demonstration of storytelling.

Participants asked to prepare a short, traditional tale (3–5 minutes) for presentation at the next session.

Session 3   Stories told by participants.

General and constructive criticism offered by workshop leader and other participants. The leader must see that comments or criticisms are constructive and of such a nature that everyone can learn from them.

Remainder of time used to discuss any problems arising from the participants' experience in preparing their stories.

Session 4   Program planning.

Administration.

Model story hour by workshop leader.

Each participant asked to prepare a longer and more complex story (7–10 minutes) for presentation at the next session.

Session 5   Participants tell their stories and discuss their programs. General and constructive criticism offered by workshop leader and participants.

Evaluation of the workshop

Depending on the size of the group, it may be necessary to have additional sessions so that everyone has a chance to tell a story. If possible, the workshop leader should observe each participant as he or she tells a story to a group of children. This also presents an opportunity for the workshop leader to discuss in private any specific criticisms or suggestions he or she may have for the beginning storyteller.

One-day workshops planned for a larger audience with a wider range of experience often include several resource persons in addition to the workshop leader. (Figure 13.) A suggested program for such a workshop follows.

*Morning Session*

Keynote speaker. Have an inspirational speaker who will set the tone. Divide the audience into small interest groups, such as:

1. Outreach Storytelling
2. The Black Heritage in Storytelling
3. Poetry in the Story Hour
4. Folktales for Children 8 Years of Age and Older
5. The Illustrator as Storyteller

Each group must have a specialist who will direct the discussion and act as resource person and demonstration storyteller. Allow at least 1½ hours for the morning interest groups.

FIGURE 13. Ellin Greene presents "The Illustrator As Storyteller" to students at Louisiana State University School of Library and Information Science. (Photograph courtesy of LSU Public Relations Office.)

*Luncheon*

*Afternoon Session*

The interest groups can be repeated so that each participant can hear about two different aspects of storytelling, or the workshop can be arranged so that the participants stay in the same group all day. This allows the group to go into greater depth of subject matter and also to have more time for demonstration and audience participation. Time should be allowed for a question and answer period. An alternative plan is to have shorter afternoon interest groups and to end the workshop with a storytelling demonstration by the various specialist leaders to the entire audience.

## Planning a Storytelling Festival

Storytelling festivals are inspirational in nature and are usually planned for a large audience with varying storytelling experience. They may or may not include workshops for the audience.

### Selection of Storytellers and Stories

Consider only the best storytellers. They may be members of the staff or invited guests. (The latter may necessitate financial expenditures.) Select storytellers who have different styles and techniques, so that the program will have variety both in content and length of stories. The stories should represent the best versions of folktales and the finest literature.

### The Physical Setting

Select a quiet room that can be made attractive and that has good acoustics. Use flowers and beautifully illustrated books as background. Arrange the books in groups, perhaps by theme, and vary the sizes and colors within each group. Simplicity and an uncluttered appearance are necessary.

Arrange the books from which the stories will be told on the story-hour table with a bowl of fresh flowers and the wishing candle, if one is to be used.

Arrange the chairs so that everyone can see the storyteller. Avoid using small, juvenile chairs for adult audiences. This is not "cute"—it is very uncomfortable for adults and makes some of them self-conscious.

# CUMBAYAH '87
## Schedule of Events

FRIDAY, MAY 15 — 8:00 p.m.                                    Adults $10.00
    Bickford Park High School               Students & Seniors $8.00
    777 Bloor St. W., Toronto                         Children $5.00

*SINGIN' OUR STORY — The Journey from Africa to the New World in song.*
    *Performed by:*   Voices of Joy — Peggy Downes, director
                     La Petite Musicale — Lindy Burgess, director
                     Yvonne Francis - Steel Pan;
                     Sethalbi Taunyne - Drummer.

    *Narrator:*      Amah Harris and Sethalbi Taunyne

    *Written and*
    *Directed by:*    Maud Fuller

---

SATURDAY, MAY 16 — 8:00 p.m.                                  Adults $10.00
    Bickford Park High School               Students & Seniors $8.00
    777 Bloor St. W., Toronto                         Children $5.00

*DANCE A STORY — The Story of Carnival.*
                  *Produced and Performed by Chissamba Chiyuka Arts Inc.*

    *Guest Artists:*   Richardo Keens Douglas; Pan Man Pat; Maureen Coard;
                     Doreen Rigby; Anne Marie Antoine;
                     La Petite Musicale; Earl Cox; Winston Cummings.
                     Sethalbi Taunyne - Drummer.

    *Script:*       Jean Sheen

    *Choreography:*  Aloma Mendoza; Laureen Tobias; Jean Sheen

    *Costumes,*
    *Sound,*
    *Lighting:*     Garnett Neblette

     Opening : Cannes Brûles        Scene 3 : Monday Night Jump-up
     Scene 1 : Carnival in Earlier Times  Scene 4 : Tuesday Carnival
     Scene 2 : Jour Ouvert          Scene 5 : Las Lap
           : Monday Carnival          Finale

---

SUNDAY, MAY 17 — 3:00 p.m.                                    Admission Free
    First Baptist Church
    101 Huron Street, Toronto

*THE RENAISSANCE CHOIR — Paul Keen Douglas*

---

SATURDAY, MAY 30 — 10:00 a.m. - 4:00 p.m.                            $30.00
    Parkdale Library
    1303 Queen St. W., Toronto

*WORKSHOP — Paul Keens Douglas (Tim Tim)*
        The oral tradition, writing and performance.
        The storyteller and his craft.
        Presented by The Storytellers School of Toronto.

FIGURE 14. Program for CUMBAYAH '87, a festival of black heritage and storytelling held May 11–30, 1987.

## A(UGUSTA) BAKER'S DOZEN
### Schedule of Events

FRIDAY, APRIL 3

9:30 a.m.–11:30 a.m.
Storytelling for area fourth grade students.

3:30 p.m.–5:00 p.m.
Workshop on Illustration of Children's Books—
Ann Grifalconi *The World Through Her Eyes:*
*A Cross Cultural Experience*
By advanced registration
Davis College, College of Library and Information Science, USC

7:30 p.m.
First Augusta Baker Lecture
Marcia Brown, Lecturer—*Marcia Brown: Communicating*
Williams-Brice College of Nursing, USC

SATURDAY, APRIL 4

10:30 a.m.–1:00 p.m.
*Storytelling for the Family* featuring:
Augusta Baker, Marcia Brown,
Rita Cox, Ellin Greene
and other nationally known storytellers.
Sale and autographing of authors' books—
Robert Mills Historic House and Park

FIGURE 15. A(ugusta) Baker's Dozen—A Celebration of Stories, sponsored by Richland County Public Library, the College of Library and Information Science at the University of South Carolina, and the South Carolina State Library with support from the Friends of the Richland County Public Library, Inc. April 3–4, 1987.

## The Program

Each segment of the program should not last more than an hour and a half. The person who presides should set the stage with a few appropriate remarks about storytelling and the program, and each story-teller should be introduced by a short characterization of either the story to be told or the storyteller. Give the program dignity and integrity. No coy, "let's pretend we are children" remarks.

Plan time at the end of the program for the audience to chat informally with the storytellers.

The programs of two actual storytelling festivals (with workshops) are shown in Figures 14 and 15.

# Appendix 2
# Sources for the Storyteller

## The Art of Storytelling
### Books and Excerpts from Books

Abrahams, Roger D. *African Folktales*. New York: Pantheon, 1983.

———. *Afro-American Folktales*. New York: Pantheon, 1984.

Afanas'ev, Alekandr. *Russian Fairy Tales*. Translated by Norbert Guteman. Commentary by Roman Jakobson. New York: Pantheon, 1945. (Reissued 1976.)

Andersen, Hans Christian. *The Complete Fairy Tales and Stories*. Translated from the Danish by Erik Christian Haugaard. New York: Doubleday, 1974.

———. *Hans Christian Andersen: Eighty Fairy Tales*. Translated by R. P. Keigwin. Introduction by Elias Bredsdorff. Illustrated by Vilhelm Pedersen and Lorenz Frolich. New York: Pantheon. 1982.

Arnott, Kathleen. *African Myths and Legends*. Illustrated by Joan Kiddell-Monroe. New York: Oxford University Press, 1962.

Asbjørnsen, Peter Christian, and Moe, Jørgen. *Norwegian Folk Tales*. New York: Pantheon, 1982.

Ausebel, Nathan. *A Treasury of Jewish Folklore*. New York: Crown, 1948.

Barron, Pamela Petrick, and Burley, Jennifer Q. *Jump over the Moon Selected Professional Readings*. New York: Holt, 1984. See especially, Part 10: Storytelling.

Barton, Bob. *Tell Me Another: Storytelling and Reading Aloud at Home, at School and in the Community*. Markham, Ont.: Pembroke, 1986.

Bauman, Richard. *Verbal Art as Performance*. Rowley, Mass.: Newbury, 1977.

Bettelheim, Bruno. *The Uses of Enchantment: The Meaning and Importance of Fairy Tales*. New York: Knopf, 1976.

Bierhorst, John. *The Mythology of North America*. New York: Morrow, 1985.

Briggs, Katherine. *British Folk Tales*. New York: Pantheon, 1977. A selection from the four-volume *A Dictionary of British Folk-tales* (London: Routledge & Kegan Paul, 1970–1971), with new introductions.

————. *The Fairies in Tradition and Literature.* Chicago: University of Chicago, 1967.

Brown, Marcia. *Lotus Seeds: Children, Pictures, and Books.* New York: Scribner, 1986.

Bryant, Sara Cone. *How to Tell Stories to Children.* Reprint of 1924 edition. Detroit: Gale, 1973.

Bushnaq, Inea. *Arab Folktales.* New York: Pantheon, 1986.

Butler, Dorothy. *Babies Need Books.* New York: Atheneum, 1982.

————. *Cushla and Her Books.* Boston: Horn Book, 1980.

Calvino, Italo. *Italian Folktales.* New York: Harcourt, 1980.

Campbell, Joseph. "Folkloristic Commentary." In *The Complete Grimm's Fairy Tales*, pp. 833–863. New York: Pantheon, 1976.

Chambers, Aidan. "Storytelling and Reading Aloud." In his *Introducing Books to Children*, 2nd ed., completely revised and expanded, pp. 129–156. Boston: Horn Book, 1983.

Chukovsky, Kornei. *From Two to Five.* Translated and edited by Miriam Morton. Berkeley: University of California Press, 1963.

Clarkson, Atelia, and Cross, Gilbert. *World Folktales: A Scribner Resource Collection.* New York: Scribner, 1980.

Colum, Padraic. "Introduction." In *The Complete Grimm's Fairy Tales*, pp. xi–xvii. New York: Pantheon, 1976.

Colwell, Eileen. *Storytelling.* London: Bodley Head, 1980.

Cook, Elizabeth. *The Ordinary and the Fabulous: An Introduction to Myths, Legends, and Fairy Tales*, 2nd ed. New York: Cambridge University Press, 1976.

Courlander, Harold. *Treasury of African Folklore.* New York: Crown, 1975.

————. *Treasury of Afro-American Folklore.* New York: Crown, 1976.

Crossley-Holland, Kevin. *The Norse Myths.* New York: Pantheon, 1980.

De la Mare, Walter. *Animal Stories.* New York: Scribner, 1940, o.p. The introduction traces the development of the animal folktale.

Dorson, Richard M. *America in Legend: Folklore from the Colonial Period to the Present.* New York: Pantheon, 1973.

Dundes, Alan, ed. *Cinderella: A Casebook.* New York: Garland, 1982.

Erdoes, Richard, and Ortz, Alfonso. *American Indian Myths and Legends.* New York: Pantheon, 1984.

Favat, F. André. *Child and Tale: The Origins of Interest.* Urbana, Ill.: National Council of Teachers of English, 1977.

Gardner, Howard. "Literature." In *The Arts and Human Development*, pp. 198–215. New York: Wiley, 1973.

Glassie, Henry. *Irish Folktales*. New York: Pantheon, 1985.

Grimm, Jacob, and Grimm, Wilhelm. *The Complete Grimm's Fairy Tales*. New York: Pantheon, 1976.

Hamilton, Edith. *Mythology*. Boston: Little, 1942.

Harrell, John. *Origins and Early Traditions of Storytelling*. Kensington, Calif.: York House, 1983.

Hazard, Paul. *Books, Children and Men*, 5th ed. Boston: Horn Book, 1983.

Huck, Charlotte S. *Children's Literature in the Elementary School*. New York: Holt, 1987.

Johnson, Edna; Sickels, Evelyn; and Sayers, Frances Clarke. *Anthology of Children's Literature*, 5th ed. Boston: Houghton, 1977. Introductions to the individual sections and Appendix A.

Kimmel, Margaret Mary, and Segal, Elizabeth. *For Reading Out Loud! A Guide to Sharing Books with Children*. Foreword by Betsy Byars. New York: Delacorte, 1983.

Luthi, Max. *The European Folktale: Form and Nature*. Translated by John D. Niles. Philadelphia: Institute for the Study of Human Issues, 1982.

———. *Once Upon a Time: On the Nature of Fairy Tales*. Bloomington: Indiana University Press, 1976.

MacDonald, Margaret Read. *Twenty Tellable Tales*. New York: Wilson, 1986.

Manheim, Ralph. *Grimm's Tales for Young and Old: The Complete Stories*. New York: Doubleday, 1977.

Meigs, Cornelia. *A Critical History of Children's Literature*. New York: Macmillan, 1969.

Norton, Eloise Speed, ed. *Folk Literature of the British Isles: Readings for Librarians, Teachers and Those Who Work with Children and Young Adults*. Metuchen, N.J.: Scarecrow, 1978.

Noy, Dov, ed. *Folktales of Israel*. Folktales of the World series. Chicago: University of Chicago Press, 1963.

Opie, Iona, and Opie, Peter. *The Classic Fairy Tales*. New York: Oxford University Press, 1974.

Pellowski, Anne. *The Story Vine: A Source Book of Unusual and Easy-to-Tell Stories from Around the World*. Illustrated by Lynn Sweat. New York: Macmillan, 1984.

———. *The World of Storytelling*. New York: Bowker, 1977.

Ross, Mabel H., and Walker, Barbara K. *"On Another Day . . ."*: *Tales Told among the Nkundo of Zaire*. Metuchen, N.J.: Shoe String, 1979.

Sawyer, Ruth. *My Spain: A Storyteller's Year of Collecting.* New York: Viking, 1967, o.p.

————. *The Way of the Storyteller.* New York: Viking, 1942, 1962; rev. ed. Penguin, 1977.

Sayers, Frances Clarke. "From Me to You" and "The Storyteller's Art." In her *Summoned by Books: Essays and Speeches,* pp. 93–98, 99–106. New York: Viking, 1965, o.p.

Shedlock, Marie. *The Art of the Story-Teller,* 3rd ed. New York: Dover, 1951.

Sherlock, Philip. *West Indian Folk-Tales.* Illustrated by Joan Kiddell Monroe. New York: Oxford University Press, 1966, 1978.

Smith, Lillian. "The Art of the Fairy Tale." In her *The Unreluctant Years: A Critical Approach to Children's Literature,* pp. 44–63. Chicago: American Library Association, 1953, o.p.

Sutherland, Zena. *Children and Books,* 7th ed. Glenview, Ill.: Scott, Foresman, 1986.

Tashjian, Virginia A. *Juba This and Juba That: Story Hour Stretches for Large or Small Groups.* Boston: Little, 1969.

————. *With a Deep Sea Smile: Story Hour Stretches for Large or Small Groups.* Boston: Little, 1974.

Taylor, Denny, and Strickland, Dorothy S. *Family Storybook Reading.* Exeter, N.H.: Heinemann, 1986.

Thompson, Stith. *The Folktale.* Berkeley: University of California Press, 1977.

Trelease, Jim. *The Read-Aloud Handbook.* Rev. ed. New York: Viking/Penguin, 1985.

Tyler, Royall. *Japanese Tales.* New York: Pantheon, 1986.

Yolen, Jane. *Touch Magic: Fantasy, Faerie and Folklore in the Literature of Childhood.* New York: Philomel, 1981.

Zipes, Jack. *Don't Bet on the Prince: Contemporary Feminist Fairy Tales in North America and England.* New York: Methuen, 1986.

Ziskind, Sylvia. *Telling Stories to Children.* New York: Wilson, 1976.

## Bibliographies and Indexes

American Library Association. Association for Library Service to Children. *Storytelling: Readings/Bibliographies/Resources.* Chicago: American Library Association, 1978.

Brewton, John E., and Brewton, Sara W. *Index to Children's Poetry.* New York: Wilson, 1942. First Supplement, 1954; Second Supplement, 1965; Third Supplement, 1975.

Briggs, Katherine. *An Encyclopedia of Fairies*. New York: Pantheon, 1976.

Cathon, Laura, ed. *Stories to Tell Children: A Selected List*, 8th ed. Pittsburgh: University of Pittsburgh Press for Carnegie Library of Pittsburgh, 1974.

Coughlan, Margaret, ed. *Folklore from Africa to the United States: An Annotated Bibliography*. Washington, D.C.: Library of Congress, 1976, o.p.

Eastman, Mary. *Index to Fairy Tales, Myths and Legends*. Boston: Faxon, 1926. Supplements 1 and 2. Boston: Faxon, 1937, 1952, o.p.

Greene, Ellin, and Shannon, George. *Storytelling: A Selected Annotated Bibliography*. New York: Garland, 1986.

Haviland, Virginia. "Storytelling," "Folktales, Myths and Legends," and "Poetry and Children." In her *Children's Literature: A Guide to Reference Sources*, pp. 183–201, 201–226, 235–241. Washington, D.C.: Library of Congress, 1966. Also "Storytelling," "Folktales, Myths and Legends," and "Poetry and Children." In the first supplement to her *Children's Literature: A Guide to Reference Sources*, pp. 121–122, 123–132, 134–136. Washington, D.C.: Library of Congress, 1972.

Hunt, Mary Alice, ed. *A Multimedia Approach to Children's Literature*, 3rd ed. Foreword by Ellin Greene. Chicago: American Library Association, 1983.

Iarusso, Marilyn. *Stories: A List of Stories to Tell and to Read Aloud*, 7th ed. New York: New York Public Library, 1977.

Ireland, Norma. *Index to Fairy Tales, 1949–1972, Including Folklore, Legends and Myths in Collections*. Metuchen, N.J.: Scarecrow, 1973.

———. *Index to Fairy Tales, 1973–1977, Including Folklore, Legends and Myths in Collections*. Metuchen, N.J.: Scarecrow, 1985.

Kohn, Rita. *Mythology for Young People: A Reference Guide*. New York: Garland, 1985.

Leach, Maria, ed. *The Standard Dictionary of Folklore, Mythology and Legends*. 2 vols. New York: Harper, 1984.

MacDonald, Margaret Read. *The Storyteller's Sourcebook: A Subject, Title and Motif Index to Folklore Collections for Children*. Detroit: Neal-Schuman/Gale Research, 1982.

Rooth, Anna Birgitta. *The Cinderella Cycle*. New York: Arno, 1980.

Shannon, George W. B. *Folk Literature and Children: An Annotated Bibliography of Secondary Materials*. Westport, Conn.: Greenwood, 1981.

Ullom, Judith C. *Folklore of the North American Indian: An Annotated Bibliography*. Washington, D.C.: Library of Congress, 1969.

Ziegler, Elsie B. *Folklore: An Annotated Bibliography and Index to Single Editions*. New York: Faxon, 1973.

## Folktales and Fairy Tales

### Collections

Baker, Augusta. *The Golden Lynx and Other Tales.* Philadelphia: Lippincott, 1960, o.p. A selection of folktales from many lands.

Belpré, Pura. *The Tiger and the Rabbit, and Other Tales.* Philadelphia: Lippincott, 1965, o.p. Folktales from Puerto Rico.

Bierhorst, John. *The Monkey's Haircut and Other Stories Told by the Maya.* New York: Morrow, 1986. An unusual collection of folktales that includes myths, just-so stories, witch stories, and animal tales. Contains an excellent introduction, sources, variants, and bibliography.

———. *The Naked Bear: Folktales of the Iroquois.* New York: Morrow, 1987. A skillfully edited collection of excellent stories for telling.

———. *The Whistling Skeleton: American Indian Tales of the Supernatural.* Collected by George Bird Grinnell. New York: Four Winds, 1982. Stories from the Pawnee, the Blackfeet, and the Cheyenne. The informative foreword deepens understanding of the traditions and customs of the three tribes.

Bryan, Ashley. *Beat the Story Drum, Pum-Pum.* Retold and illustrated by Ashley Bryan. New York: Atheneum, 1980, o.p. African tales told with rhythm, humor, and vigor.

———. *Lion and the Ostrich Chicks and Other African Tales.* Illustrated by Ashley Bryan. New York: Atheneum, 1986. Four stories that represent different African peoples—Masai, Bushman, Angola, and Hausa.

———. *The Ox of the Wonderful Horns and Other African Folktales.* New York: Atheneum, 1971, o.p.

Carrick, Valery. *Picture Tales from the Russian.* New York: Dover, 1967, o.p.

Chase, Richard. *Grandfather Tales.* Boston: Houghton, 1948. Tales collected from the southern Appalachian folk and retold with local idioms.

———. *Jack Tales.* Boston: Houghton, 1943. Appalachian tales centered around the character Jack.

Coatsworth, Emerson, and Coatsworth, David. *The Adventures of Nanabush: Ojibway Indian Stories.* New York: Atheneum, 1980, o.p. These sixteen stories told by five Native American storytellers were recorded in the 1930s by Emerson Coatsworth, a historical field researcher, and later completed by his son David.

Colwell, Eileen. *The Magic Umbrella and Other Stories for Telling.* London: Bodley Head, 1981.

Courlander, Harold. *Cow-tail Switch and Other West African Stories.* New York: Holt, 1947, 1987.

Crossley-Holland, Kevin. *The Faber Book of Northern Folk-Tales.* New York: Faber, 1981.

———. *The Fox and the Cat: Animal Tales from Grimm.* Illustrated by Susan Varley. New York: Morrow, 1985. Short, familiar stories that can be told as encores to a program.

D'Aulaire, Ingri, and Parin, Edgar. *East of the Sun and West of the Moon: Twenty-one Norwegian Folk Tales.* New York: Viking, 1969, o.p.

Faulkner, William J. *The Days When the Animals Talked: Black American Folk Tales and How They Came to Be.* Illustrated by Troy Stowell. Chicago: Follett, 1977, o.p. Slave tales as well as animal stories told without dialect. Introductions are a good base for the storyteller.

Finger, Charles. *Tales from Silver Lands.* New York: Doubleday, 1924. Contains several chilling stories from South America that are excellent for the Halloween story hour. A Newbery Award book.

Gág, Wanda. *Tales from Grimm* and *More Tales from Grimm.* New York: Coward, 1936, 1947, o.p.

Garner, Alan. *Alan Garner's Book of British Fairy Tales.* Illustrated by Derek Collard. New York: Delacorte, 1985. Both familiar and unfamiliar folktales told and illustrated with strength and power.

———. *A Bag of Moonshine.* Illustrated by Patrick James Lynch. New York: Delacorte, 1986. Stories of boggarts and hobgoblins chosen from the folklore of England and Wales.

———. *The Lad of the Gad.* New York: Philomel, 1981, o.p. Five Gaelic stories, four drawn from *Popular Tales of the West Highlands*, by J. F. Campbell, and one based on an Irish manuscript, "The Adventures of the Children of the King of Norway."

Greene, Ellin. *Midsummer Magic: A Garland of Stories, Charms, and Recipes.* New York: Lothrop, 1977, o.p. (Available from the author.)

Grimm, Jakob, and Grimm, Wilhelm. *About Wise Men and Simpletons.* Translated from the German by Elizabeth Shub. New York: Macmillan, 1971.

———. *The Brothers Grimm: Popular Folk Tales.* Newly translated by Brian Alderson. Illustrated by Michael Foreman. Doubleday, 1978.

———. *Household Stories of the Brothers Grimm.* Translated from the German by Lucy Crane. New York: Dover, 1963.

———. *The Juniper Tree and Other Tales from Grimm.* Selected by Lore Segal and Maurice Sendak. Translated from the German by Lore Segal and Randall Jarrell. New York: Farrar, 1973.

Hamilton, Virginia. *The People Could Fly: American Black Folktales.* Illustrated by Leo Dillon and Diane Dillon. New York: Knopf, 1985. Twenty-four selections that represent the main body of American black folklore. Includes the animal stories, John stories, and slave tales.

Harris, Christie. *Mouse Woman and the Mischief-Makers.* New York: Atheneum, 1977.

———. *The Trouble with Adventurers.* New York: Atheneum, 1982. Stories from the native people of the Pacific Northwest.

Harris, Joel Chandler. *Jump! The Adventures of Brer Rabbit.* Adapted by Van Dyhe Parks and Malcolm Jones. Illustrated by Barry Moser. New York: Harcourt, 1986. The adaptors-retellers have eliminated the fictional character Uncle Remus and use standard English in this collection for younger children.

Haviland, Virginia. *The Fairy Tale Treasury.* New York: Coward, 1972. Thirty-two of the best-loved tales for young children.

———. *Favorite Fairy Tales Told around the World.* Illustrated by S. C. Schindler. Boston: Little, 1985. A selection from the 16-volume series. Retold in simple language for children to read for themselves.

He, Liyi. *The Spring of Butterflies: And Other Folktales of China's Minority Peoples.* Translated by He Liyi. Edited by Neil Philip. Paintings by Pan Aiqing and Li Zhao. New York: Lothrop, 1985. Traditional stories of the Tibetan, Thai, Uighur, and Bai peoples who live in China.

Jacobs, Joseph. *English Fairy Tales.* New York: Dover, 1898.

Jagendorf, M. A., and Weng, Virginia. *The Magic Boat and Other Chinese Folk Stories.* New York: Vanguard, 1980.

Jaquith, Priscilla. *Bo Rabbit Smart for True: Folktales from the Gullah.* Drawings by Ed Young. New York: Putnam, 1981. (Philomel Books.) Four hilarious stories told on the Sea Islands of Georgia and South Carolina, using a modified version of a poetic, lilting pattern of speech.

Lang, Andrew. *Blue Fairy Book.* New York: Dover, 1965.

———. *Green Fairy Book.* Edited by Brian Alderson. Illustrated by Anthony Maitland. New York: Viking, 1978.

———. *Pink Fairy Book.* Edited by Brian Alderson. Illustrated by Colin McNaughton. New York: Viking, 1982.

———. *Red Fairy Book.* Edited by Brian Alderson. Illustrated by Faith Jacques. New York: Viking, 1978.

———. *Yellow Fairy Book.* Edited by Brian Alderson. Illustrated by Erik Blegvad. New York: Viking, 1980.

Leach, Maria. *Whistle in the Graveyard: Folk Tales to Chill Your Bones.* Illustrated by Ken Rinciari. New York: Viking, 1974.

Lester, Julius. *The Knee-High Man and Other Tales.* New York: Dial, 1972.

———. *The Tales of Uncle Remus: The Adventures of Brer Rabbit.* Introduction by Augusta Baker. Illustrated by Jerry Pinkney. New York: Dial,

1987. Lester uses the voice and language of black people in what he calls "a modified contemporary southern black English." Storytellers will appreciate his concise, historical, and chronological explanation of the stories.

Literature Committee of the Association for Childhood Education International. *Told under the Green Umbrella.* New York: Macmillan, 1958, o.p.

MacManus, Seumas. *Donegal Fairy Stories.* New York: Dover, 1968.

Martin, Eva, and Gál, László. *Tales of the Far North.* New York: Dial, 1986. Twelve Canadian fairy tales, born of the marriage of French and English traditions.

Nic Leodhas, Sorche. *Heather and Broom: Tales of the Scottish Highlands.* New York: Holt, 1960, o.p.

O'Brien, Edna. *Tales for the Telling: Irish Folk and Fairy Stories.* Illustrated by Michael Foreman. New York: Atheneum, 1986.

Perrault, Charles. *Perrault's Complete Fairy Tales.* Translated from the French by A. E. Johnson. Illustrated by W. H. Robinson. New York: Dodd, 1982.

Phelps, Ethel Johnson. *The Maid of the North: Feminist Folk Tales from Around the World.* Illustrated by Lloyd Bloom. New York: Holt, 1981.

Ransome, Arthur. *Old Peter's Russian Tales.* Bridgeport, Conn.: Merrimack, 1984.

Riorden, James. *Tales from the Arabian Nights.* Illustrated by Victor G. Ambrus. New York: Macmillan, 1985.

———. *The Woman in the Moon and Other Tales of Forgotten Heroines.* Illustrated by Angela Barrett. New York: Dial, 1985.

Rockwell, Anne. *The Old Woman and Her Pig and 10 Other Stories.* New York: Crowell, 1979.

———. *The Three Bears and 15 Other Stories.* New York: Crowell, 1975.

Sadler, Catherine Edwards. *Heaven's Reward: Fairy Tales from China.* Illustrated by Cheng Mung Yun. New York: Atheneum, 1985.

———. *Treasure Mountain: Folktales from Southern China.* Illustrated by Cheng Mung Yun. New York: Atheneum, 1982.

Sanders, Scott R. *Hear the Wind Blow: American Folk Songs Retold.* Illustrated by Ponder Goembel. New York: Bradbury, 1985. The lyrics of 20 folk songs have been expanded into stories.

Schwartz, Alvin. *Scary Stories to Tell in the Dark.* Collected from American Folklore by Alvin Schwartz. Drawings by Stephen Gammell. Philadelphia: Lippincott, 1981. See other collections by this author.

Schwartz, Howard. *Elijah's Violin and Other Jewish Fairy Tales.* Illustrated by Linda Heller. New York: Harper, 1983, o.p.

————. *Miriam's Tambourine: Jewish Folktales around the World.* New York: Seth Press, 1986.

Serwadda, W. Moses. *Songs and Stories from Uganda.* Transcribed and edited by Hewitt Pantalconi. Illustrated by Leo Dillon and Diane Dillon. New York: Crowell, 1974.

Sherlock, Philip M. *West Indian Folktales.* New York: Oxford University Press, 1978 (reprint).

Singer, Isaac B. *The Fools of Chelm and Their History.* Translated from the Yiddish by Elizabeth Shub. Illustrated by Uri Shulevitz. New York: Farrar, 1973.

Stoutenburg, Adrien. *American Tall Tales.* New York: Penguin, 1976.

Timpanelli, Gioia. *Tales from the Roof of the World: Folktales of Tibet.* Illustrated by Elizabeth Kelly Lockwood. New York: Viking, 1984.

Vuong, Lynette Dyer. *The Brocaded Slipper and Other Vietnamese Tales.* Illustrated by Vo-Dinh Mai. Reading, Mass.: Addison-Wesley, 1982, o.p. Vietnamese variants of familiar folktales such as "Cinderella" and "The Frog Prince."

Williamson, Duncan. *Fireside Tales of the Traveller Children. Twelve Scottish Stories.* Illustrated by Alan B. Herriot. New York: Crown, 1985.

Wolkstein, Diane. *The Magic Orange Tree and Other Haitian Folktales.* Drawings by Elsa Henriqueg. New York: Knopf, 1978.

Yolen, Jane. *Favorite Folktales from Around the World.* New York: Pantheon, 1986. One hundred sixty tales from more than 40 different cultures. Excellent introduction.

## Picture-Book Editions

Aardema, Verna. *Bimwili and the Zimwi.* Illustrated by Susan Meddaugh. New York: Dial, 1985. "A tale from Zanzibar" in which the little girl Bimwili outwits an ogre.

————. *Who's in Rabbit's House?* Pictures by Leo Dillon and Diane Dillon. New York: Dial, 1977. A humorous Masai tale for younger children.

————. *Why Mosquitoes Buzz in People's Ears.* Illustrated by Leo Dillon and Diane Dillon. New York: Dial, 1975.

Asbjørnsen, Peter C., and Moe, Jørgen E. *The Three Billy Goats Gruff.* Illustrated by Marcia Brown. New York: Harcourt, 1957, o.p.

Bang, Betsy. *The Old Woman and the Rice Thief.* Illustrated by Molly Bang. New York: Greenwillow, 1978.

Bang, Molly Garrett. *Wiley and the Hairy-Man.* Adapted from an American Folktale. New York: Macmillan, 1976. How Wiley and his mother trick the Hairy-Man.

Belpré, Pura. *Perez and Martina.* Illustrated by Carlos Sanchez. New York: Warne, 1961, o.p.

Brooke, L. Leslie. *The Golden Goose Book.* Illustrated by L. Leslie Brooke. New York: Warne, 1905, o.p.

———. *Stories from the Golden Goose Book.* New York, Warne, 1987.

Brown, Marcia. *Once a Mouse.* Illustrated by Marcia Brown. New York: Scribner, 1961. A fable about big and little, set in India.

Bryan, Ashley. *The Cat's Purr.* New York: Atheneum, 1985. An old West Indian folktale, about Cat and his drum.

———. *The Dancing Granny.* New York: Atheneum, 1977. Granny Anika and Spider Ananse become dancing partners in this West Indian story.

Conover, Chris. *Froggie Went A-Courting.* Retold and illustrated by Chris Conover. New York: Farrar, 1986. A retelling of an Elizabethan nursery rhyme.

Cooper, Susan. *The Silver Cow: A Welsh Tale.* Illustrated by Warwick Hutton. New York: Atheneum, 1983. A story about the greed of a crafty farmer and the revenge of the magic people, the Tylwyth Teg.

Crompton, Anne. *The Winter Wife: An Abenaki Folktale.* Illustrated by Robert Parker. Boston: Little, 1975.

Dayrell, Elphinstone. *Why the Sun and Moon Live in the Sky.* Illustrated by Blair Lent. Boston: Houghton, 1968, o.p.

de Gerez, Toni. *Louhi, Witch of North Farm: A Story from Finland's Epic Poem the Kalevala.* Illustrated by Barbara Cooney. New York: Viking, 1986. A vividly retold tale from "the Land of Heroes."

Domanska, Janina. *A Scythe, a Rooster, and a Cat.* New York: Greenwillow, 1981. A retelling of a Russian folktale.

Gág, Wanda, and Tomes, Margot. *Jorinda and Joringel.* New York: Coward, 1978.

Galdone, Joanna. *The Tailypo: A Ghost Story.* Illustrated by Paul Galdone. New York: Seabury, 1977.

Galdone, Paul. *What's in Fox's Sack?* New York: Clarion, 1982. A retelling, for younger children, of an old English folktale.

Gerstein, Mordicai. *The Seal Mother.* New York: Dial, 1986.

Grimm, Jakob, and Grimm, Wilhelm. *The Devil and the Three Golden Hairs.* Retold and illustrated by Nonny Hogrogian. New York: Knopf, 1983.

———. *The Elves and the Shoemaker.* Retold and illustrated by Bernadette Watts. New York: Holt, 1986.

———. *The Glass Mountain.* Retold and illustrated by Nonny Hogrogian. New York: Knopf, 1985.

———. *Little Red Riding Hood.* Retold and illustrated by Trina Schart Hyman. New York: Holiday House, 1983.

———. *The Seven Ravens.* Translated from the German by Elizabeth D. Crawford. Illustrated by Lisbeth Zwerger. New York: Morrow, 1981.

———. *The Shoemaker and the Elves.* Illustrated by Adrienne Adams. New York: Scribner, 1960.

———. *The Sleeping Beauty.* Retold and illustrated by Trina Schart Hyman. New York: Little, 1977.

———. *The Sleeping Beauty.* Retold and illustrated by Warwick Hutton. New York: Macmillan, 1979.

———. *Snow-White and the Seven Dwarfs.* Illustrated by Randall Jarrell. Translated from the German by Nancy Burkert. New York: Farrar, 1972.

———. *The Wolf and the Seven Little Kids.* Illustrated by Felix Hoffman. New York: Harcourt, 1959, o.p.

Haley, Gail E. *Jack and the Bean Tree.* New York: Crown, 1986.

———. *A Story, A Story: An African Tale.* New York: Atheneum, 1970.

Heyer, Marilee. *The Weaving of a Dream: A Chinese Folktale.* New York: Viking, 1986.

Hodges, Margaret. *The Little Humpbacked Horse.* New York: Farrar, 1980, o.p. Based on a story by the Russian writer Peter Pavlovich Yashov.

Hooks, William H. *Moss Gown.* Illustrated by Donald Carrick. New York: Clarion, 1987. A traditional English tale that preserves elements of the King Lear story and "Cinderella," as told in the tidewater section of eastern North Carolina.

Jacobs, Joseph. *King of the Cats.* Illustrated by Paul Galdone. New York: Clarion, 1980. A story for Halloween shivers.

———. *Tom Tit Tot.* Illustrated by Evaline Ness. New York: Scribner, 1965, o.p.

Lang, Andrew, reteller. *Aladdin and the Wonderful Lamp.* Illustrated by Errol Le Cain. New York: Viking, 1981.

Langston, Jane. *The Hedgehog Boy: A Latvian Folktale.* Illustrated by Ilse Plume. New York: Harper, 1985.

Lee, Jeanne M. *Toad Is the Uncle of Heaven: A Vietnamese Folktale.* New York: Holt, 1985. How it came to be that one day the King of Heaven called an ugly toad "Uncle."

Marshak, Samuel, reteller. *The Month-Brothers: A Slavic Tale.* Translated from the Russian by Thomas P. Whitney. Illustrated by Diane Stanley. New York: Morrow, 1983. A traditional Czechoslovakian story about a little girl who sees all the 12 months of the year at once.

Mosel, Arlene. *The Funny Little Woman.* Illustrated by Blair Lent. New

York: Dutton, 1972. A Japanese folktale about a little old woman who likes to laugh, and how she escapes from the wicked *oni* and becomes famous for her rice dumplings.

Myers, Walter Dean. *Mr. Monkey and the Gotcha Bird: An Original Tale.* Illustrated by Leslie Morrill. New York: Delacorte, 1984. A humorous story that combines African and Caribbean folktale motifs told in rhythmic language.

Orgel, Doris. *Godfather Cat and Mousie.* Retold after the Brothers Grimm. Illustrated by Ann Schweninger. New York: Macmillan, 1986. Cat and Mouse set up housekeeping and Cat steals the pot of cream hidden in the church. A Haitian variant is "Uncle Bouqui and Godfather Ti-Malice."

Pevear, Richard. *Mister Cat-and-a-Half.* Illustrated by Robert Rayevsky. New York: Macmillan, 1986. A delightful Ukrainian folktale about Mistress Fox and her lazy, overfed husband, Mister Cat-and-a-half.

Rogasky, Barbara. *The Water of Life: A Tale from the Brothers Grimm.* New York: Holiday, 1986. The youngest son finds the Water of Life and helps save his father.

San Souci, Robert D. *The Enchanted Tapestry.* Illustrated by Lázló Gál. New York: Dial, 1987.

———. *Song of Sedna.* Illustrated by Daniel San Souci. New York: Doubleday, 1981. An Eskimo tale.

Sawyer, Ruth. *Journey Cake, Ho!* Illustrated by Robert McCloskey. New York: Viking, 1953. The American variant of "The Gingerbread Boy."

Shannon, George. *The Piney Woods Peddler.* Illustrated by Nancy Tafuri. New York: Greenwillow, 1981. An original tale that uses elements of traditional American swapping songs.

Shute, Linda. *Momotaro, the Peach Boy: A Traditional Japanese Tale.* New York: Lothrop, 1986.

Steptoe, John. *Mufaro's Beautiful Daughters: An African Tale.* New York: Lothrop, 1987. An original story inspired by a folktale published in 1895 in Theal's *Kaffir Folktales.*

Whitney, Thomas P. *Vasilisa the Beautiful.* Illustrated by Nonny Hogrogian. New York: Macmillan, 1970. The Russian Cinderella.

Wolkstein, Diane. *The Red Lion: A Persian Story.* New York: Crowell, 1977.

———. *White Wave: A Chinese Tale.* Illustrated by Ed Young. New York: Crowell, 1979.

Yagawa, Sumilko. *The Crane Wife.* Translation from the Japanese by Katherine Paterson. Illustrated by Suekichi Akaba. New York: Morrow, 1981.

Zelensky, Paul O. *Rumpelstiltskin: From the German of the Brothers Grimm.* New York: Dutton, 1986.

Zemach, Harve. *Duffy and the Devil: A Cornish Tale.* Illustrated by Margot Zemach. New York: Farrar, 1973.

Zemach, Margot. *The Little Red Hen: An Old Story.* New York: Farrar, 1983. The classic nursery story reinterpreted through humorous pictures.

## Fables, Tall Tales, Myths, Legends, and Hero Tales

### Collections

Aesop. *Aesop's Fables.* Illustrated by Michael Hague. New York: Holt, 1985.

———. *Aesop's Fables.* Illustrated by Heidi Holden. New York: Viking, 1981.

———. *Tales from Aesop.* Retold and illustrated by Harold Jones. New York: Watts/Julia MacRae, 1982, o.p.

Bierhorst, John. *Black Rainbow: Legends of the Incas and Myths of Ancient Peru.* New York: Farrar, 1976.

———. *Doctor Coyote: A Native American Aesop's Fables.* Illustrated by Wendy Watson. New York: Macmillan, 1987.

———. *The Hungry Woman: Myths and Legends of the Aztecs.* New York: Morrow, 1984. Contains important and scholarly introduction which is background for the storyteller.

———. *The Ring in the Prairie.* New York: Dial, 1970.

Bryson, Bernarda. *Gilgamesh: Man's First Story.* New York: Holt, 1967, o.p.

Colum, Padraic. *The Children's Homer: The Adventures of Odysseus and the Tale of Troy.* New York: Macmillan, 1982.

Courlander, Harold. *The Crest and the Hide: And Other African Stories of Heroes, Chiefs, Bards, Hunters, Sorcerers and Common People.* New York: Coward, 1982. Twenty legends collected by the noted folklorist. With notes and sources.

De Armond, Dale. *Berry Women's Children.* New York: Greenwillow, 1985. Fables based on Eskimo myths and folklore.

Evslin, Bernard. *Signs and Wonders: Tales from the Old Testament.* Drawings by Charles Mikolaycak. New York: Macmillan, 1982.

Farmer, Penelope. *Beginnings: Creation Myths of the World.* Woodcuts by Antonio Frasconi. New York: Atheneum, 1979, o.p.

Gates, Doris. *Lord of the Sky: Zeus.* Illustrated by Robert Handville. New York: Penguin, 1982.

————. *The Warrior Goddess: Athena*. New York: Penguin, 1982.

Haviland, Virginia. *North American Legends*. New York: Philomel, 1979. Myths, legends, and tales that reflect different cultures found in North America—Indian and Eskimo tales, black American tales, European tales brought to America by immigrants, Appalachian tales, and tall tales.

Hazeltine, Alice. *Hero Tales from Many Lands*. Nashville: Abingdon, 1961, o.p.

Jaffrey, Madhur. *Seasons of Splendour: Tales, Myths and Legends of India*. Illustrated by Michael Foreman. New York: Atheneum, 1985.

Kingsley, Charles. *The Heroes*. New York: Dutton, 1963. Reprint. London: Dent, 1975.

Leach, Maria. *How the People Sang the Mountain Up*. New York: Viking, 1967, o.p.

Lurie, Alison. *The Heavenly Zoo. Legends and Tales of the Stars*. Illustrated by Monika Beisner. New York: Farrar, 1980.

Pyle, Howard. *The Merry Adventures of Robin Hood of Great Renown in Nottinghamshire*. New York: Scribner, 1911.

————. *The Story of King Arthur and His Knights*. New York: Scribner, 1933.

Robinson, Gail. *Raven the Trickster: Legends of the North American Indians*. Illustrated by Joanna Troughton. New York: Atheneum, 1982. Nine unusual and tellable tales about the mischievous "animal-god" of the early people of the northwest coast of the Pacific Ocean.

Sawyer, Ruth. *Joy to the World: Christmas Legends*. Boston: Little, 1966.

Synge, Ursula. *The Giant at the Ford and Other Legends of the Saints*. New York: Macmillan, 1980.

————. *Land of Heroes: Retelling of the Kalevala*. New York: Macmillan, 1978.

Young, Ella. *The Tangle-Coated Horse*. New York: Longmans, 1927, o.p.

## Picture-Book Editions

Calhoun, Mary. *Jack and the Whoopee Wind*. Illustrated by Dick Gackenbach. New York: Morrow, 1987. Jack sets out to tame the wind. A tall tale.

Chaucer, Geoffrey. *Chanticleer and the Fox*. Adapted and illustrated by Barbara Cooney. New York: Crowell, 1958, 1982. The story of the proud cock and the wily fox. Adapted from "Nun's Priest's Tale" in *The Canterbury Tales*.

Cooper, Susan. *The Selkie Girl*. Illustrated by Warwick Hutton. New

York: Macmillan, 1986. The Celtic legend of the marriage and parting of a seal maiden and her mortal husband.

dePaola, Tomie. *The Clown of God: An Old Story.* New York: Harcourt, 1978. The author-illustrator has given the thirteenth-century story of the juggler of Notre Dame an Italian setting.

Garfield, Leon. *King Nimrod's Tower.* Illustrated by Michael Bragg. New York: Lothrop, 1982.

———. *The Writing on the Wall.* Illustrated by Michael Bragg. New York: Lothrop, 1983.

Goble, Paul. *Buffalo Woman.* New York: Bradbury, 1984.

Haley, Gail E. *The Green Man.* New York: Scribner, 1979, o.p. The legend of the lord of the forest.

Hastings, Selina. *Sir Gawain and the Green Knight.* Illustrated by Juan Wijngaard. New York: Lothrop, 1981.

Hodges, Margaret. *Saint George and the Dragon.* A Golden Legend adapted by Margaret Hodges from Edmund Spencer's *Faerie Queene.* Illustrated by Trina Schart Hyman. New York: Little, 1984.

Hutton, Warwick. *Jonah and the Great Fish.* New York: Atheneum, 1983.

Keats, Ezra Jack. *John Henry: An American Legend.* Story and pictures by Ezra Jack Keats. New York: Pantheon, 1965. The heroic legend told in a simple, balladlike style.

Kellogg, Steven. *Pecos Bill.* New York: Morrow, 1986. A simplified telling of the tall tale that is part of our American heritage.

Lobel, Arnold. *Fables.* New York: Harper, 1980.

Mikolaycak, Charles. *Babushka: An Old Russian Folktale.* Retold and illustrated by Charles Mikolaycak. New York: Holiday House, 1984. A classic Christmas story about an old woman's search for the Christ Child.

Otsuka, Yuzo. *Suho and the White Horse: A Legend of Mongolia.* Translated from the Japanese by Ann Herring. Illustrated by Suekichi Akaba. New York: Viking, 1981.

Proddow, Penelope. *Demeter and Persephone: Homeric Hymn Number Two.* New York: Doubleday, 1972.

Steptoe, John. *The Story of Jumping Mouse.* A Native American legend retold and illustrated by John Steptoe. New York: Lothrop, 1984.

## Literary Fairy Tales

### Collections

Andersen, Hans Christian. *Ardizzone's Hans Andersen: Fourteen Classic Tales.* Translated by Stephen Corrin. Illustrated by Edward Ardizzone. New York: Atheneum, 1979.

———. *Favorite Tales of Hans Andersen*. Translated from the Danish by M. R. James. Winchester, Mass.: Faber, 1986.

———. *Hans Andersen: His Classic Fairy Tales*. Translated by Erik Haugaard. Illustrated by Michael Forman. New York: Doubleday, 1978. Eighteen favorite stories.

Babbitt, Natalie. *The Devil's Storybook*. New York: Farrar, 1974.

———. *The Devil's Other Storybook*. New York: Farrar, 1987.

Bianco, Margery Williams. *A Street of Little Shops*. Boston: Grigg, 1981. Delightful original stories set in a little country village in the 1920s.

Colum, Padraic. *The Stone of Victory and Other Tales of Padraic Colum*. New York: McGraw, 1966, o.p.

Cummings, e. e. *Fairy Tales*. New York: Harcourt, 1975.

De la Mare, Walter. *Tales Told Again*. Winchester, Mass.: Faber, 1980. Nineteen classic fairy tales retold by a literary genius.

Farjeon, Eleanor. *The Little Bookroom*. New York: Godine, 1984. The author's selection of the favorite of her own short stories for children.

Housman, Laurence. *The Rat-Catcher's Daughter: A Collection of Stories by Laurence Housman*. Selected by Ellin Greene. New York: Atheneum, 1974, o.p.

Hughes, Richard. *The Wonder Dog: The Collected Children's Stories of Richard Hughes*. New York: Morrow, 1977, o.p.

Kennedy, Richard. *Richard Kennedy: Collected Stories*. Pictures by Marcia Sewall. New York: Harper, 1987. Sixteen stories originally published separately as picture books have been gathered to form the author's first collection.

Kipling, Rudyard. *Just So Stories*. Illustrated by Safaya Salter. New York: Holt, 1987.

Peretz, I. L. *The Seven Good Years and Other Stories of I. L. Peretz*. Translated and adapted by Esther Hautzig. Philadelphia: Jewish Publication Society of America, 1984.

Perrault, Charles. *The Glass Slipper: Charles Perrault's Tales of Times Past*. Translated by John Bierhorst. Illustrated by Mitchell Miller. New York: Four Winds, 1981.

Pyle, Howard. *The Wonder Clock*. New York: Dover, 1887, 1915. Twenty-four original stories in the tradition of folktales.

Sandburg, Carl. *Rootabaga Stories*. New York: Harcourt, 1951.

Singer, Isaac B. *Stories for Children*. New York: Farrar, 1984. Thirty-six tales chosen from former collections.

———. *Zlateh the Goat and Other Stories*. New York: Harper, 1966.

Wilde, Oscar. *The Birthday of the Infanta and Other Tales*. Illustrated by Beni Montressor. New York: Atheneum, 1982, o.p.

————. *The Happy Prince and Other Stories.* New York: Dutton, 1968. Reprint. London: Dent, 1977.

Yolen, Jane. *The Girl Who Cried Flowers and Other Tales.* New York: Crowell, 1974.

### Picture-Book Editions

Andersen, Hans Christian. *The Emperor's New Clothes.* Illustrated by Dorothee Duntze. Retold by Anthea Bell. New York: Holt, 1986.

————. *The Fir Tree.* Illustrated by Nancy Burkert. New York: Harper, 1970.

————. *The Little Mermaid.* Translated from the Danish by Eva Le Gallienne. Illustrated by Edward Frascino. New York: Harper, 1971.

————. *The Nightingale.* Translated from the Danish by Eva Le Gallienne. Illustrated by Nancy Burkert. New York: Harper, 1965.

————. *The Nightingale.* Translated by Anthea Bell. Illustrated by Lisbeth Zwerger. Natick, Mass.: Picture Books, 1984.

————. *The Steadfast Tin Soldier.* Illustrated by Marcia Brown. New York: Scribner, 1953, o.p.

————. *The Swineherd.* Translated from the Danish by Anthea Bell. Illustrated by Lisbeth Zwerger. New York: Morrow, 1982.

————. *Thumbelina.* Illustrated by Adrienne Adams. New York: Scribner, 1961.

————. *Thumbelina.* Retold by Amy Ehrlich. Pictures by Susan Jeffers. New York: Dial, 1979.

————. *The Ugly Duckling.* English text by Anne Stewart. Illustrated by Monika Laimgruber. New York: Greenwillow, 1982.

————. *The Wild Swans.* Illustrated by Marcia Brown. New York: Scribner, 1963.

————. *The Wild Swans.* Retold by Amy Ehrlich. Pictures by Susan Jeffers. New York: Dial, 1981.

De la Mare, Walter. *Molly Whuppie.* Illustrated by Errol Le Cain. New York: Farrar, 1983.

Kipling, Rudyard. *The Elephant's Child.* Illustrated by Leonard Weisgard. New York: Walker, 1970.

Perrault, Charles. *Cinderella, or the Little Glass Slipper.* Illustrated by Marcia Brown. New York: Scribner, 1954.

Pyle, Howard. *King Stork.* Illustrated by Trina Schart Hyman. Boston: Little, 1973, 1986.

Stockton, Frank R. *The Bee Man of Orn.* Illustrated by Maurice Sendak. New York: Harper, 1964, 1986. The Bee Man sets out to find his original form and has many adventures.

—————. *The Griffin and the Minor Canon.* Illustrated by Maurice Sendak. New York: Harper, 1963, 1986. Middle-age children will enjoy this highly imaginative story.

Thurber, James. *Many Moons.* Illustrated by Louis Slobodkin. New York: Harcourt, 1943.

Walter, Mildred Pitts. *Brother to the Wind.* Pictures by Diane Dillon and Leo Dillon. New York: Lothrop, 1985. An original story that draws on many beliefs and symbols of the African culture.

Wilde, Oscar. *The Nightingale and the Rose.* Illustrated by Freire Wright and Michael Foreman. New York: Oxford, 1981.

Wolkstein, Diane. *The Legend of Sleepy Hollow.* Based on the story by Washington Irving. Retold by Diane Wolkstein. Illustrated by R. W. Alley. New York: Morrow, 1987.

Yolen, Jane. *The Sleeping Beauty.* Illustrated by Ruth Sanderson. New York: Knopf, 1986. A beautiful retelling of a classic love story.

## Poetry

Adoff, Arnold. *Friend Dog.* Illustrated by Troy Howell. New York: Lippincott, 1980.

—————. *The Poetry of Black America: Anthology of the Twentieth Century.* Introduction by Gwendolyn Brooks. New York: Harper, 1973.

Bauer, Caroline Feller. *Rainy Day: Stories and Poems.* New York: Lippincott, 1986.

—————. *Snowy Day: Stories and Poems.* New York: Lippincott, 1986.

Bierhorst, John. *The Sacred Path: Spells, Prayers and Power Songs of the American Indians.* New York: Morrow, 1983.

Bober, Natalie S. *Let's Pretend: Poems of Flight and Fancy.* Illustrated by Bill Bell. New York: Viking, 1986.

Bodecker, N. M. *Hurry, Hurry, Mary Dear! and Other Nonsense Poems.* New York: Macmillan, 1976.

Bontemps, Arna. *Golden Slippers: An Anthology of Negro Poetry.* New York: Harper, 1941, o.p.

—————. *Hold Fast to Your Dreams.* Chicago: Follett, 1969.

Carroll, Lewis. *The Walrus and the Carpenter.* Illustrations by Jane Breskin Zalben. New York: Holt, 1986.

Cendras, Blaise. *Shadow.* Translated and illustrated by Marcia Brown. New York: Scribner, 1982. "The eerie, shifting image of Shadow appears where there is light and fire and a storyteller to bring it to life." Powerful imagery for older children.

Chorao, Kay. *The Baby's Bedtime Book.* New York: Dutton, 1984.

—————. *The Baby's Good Morning Book.* New York: Dutton, 1986.

————. *The Baby's Lap Book.* New York: Dutton, 1987. Three beautiful collections that contain traditional rhymes as well as poems by favorite authors like Christina Rossetti, Eleanor Farjeon, and Robert Louis Stevenson.

Cole, William. *The Birds and the Beasts Were There: Animal Poems.* Cleveland: World, 1963, o.p.

————. *Poem Soup.* New York: Lippincott, 1981.

Colum, Padraic. *Roofs of Gold: Poems of Read Aloud.* New York: Macmillan, 1964, o.p.

De la Mare, Walter. *Peacock Pie.* New York: Faber, 1980.

————. *The Voice.* New York: Delacorte, 1987. Thirteen poems by the beloved poet.

de Regniers, Beatrice Schenk. *A Week in the Life of Best Friends and Other Poems of Friendship.* New York: Atheneum, 1986.

Dunning, Stephen, et al. *Reflections on a Gift of Watermelon Pickle . . . And Other Modern Verse.* Chicago: Scott, Foresman, 1966.

Farjeon, Eleanor. *Eleanor Farjeon's Poems for Children.* New York: Lippincott, 1984. The complete text of four volumes of verse by Eleanor Farjeon: *Sing for Your Supper, Over the Garden Wall, Joan's Door, Come Christmas,* and 20 poems from her *Collected Poems* heretofore published only in England.

Fisher, Aileen. *Out in the Dark and Daylight.* Illustrated by Gail Owens. New York: Harper, 1980.

Fleischman, Paul. *I Am Phoenix: Poems for Two Voices.* Illustrated by Ken Nutt. New York: Harper, 1985.

Giovanni, Nikki. *Spin a Soft Black Song: Poems for Children.* Rev. ed. New York: Hill & Wang, 1985.

Greenfield, Eloise. *Daydreamers.* Illustrated by Tom Feelings. New York: Dial, 1981.

————. *Honey, I Love and Other Love Poems.* Pictures by Diane Dillon and Leo Dillon. New York: Crowell, 1978.

Hall, Donald. *The Oxford Book of Children's Verse in America.* New York: Oxford, 1985.

Holman, Felice. *The Song in My Head and Other Poems.* New York: Scribner, 1985.

Hopkins, Lee Bennett. *Rainbows Are Made: Poems by Carl Sandburg.* Selected by Lee Bennett Hopkins. Wood engravings by Fritz Eichenberg. New York: Harcourt, 1984.

————. *The Sky Is Full of Song.* Illustrated by Dirk Zimmer. New York: Harper, 1983. An anthology that celebrates the changing of the seasons.

Hughes, Langston. *The Dream Keeper and Other Poems*. Illustrated by Helen Sewell. Introduction by Augusta Baker. New York: Knopf, 1986. The poet's own selection for young people.

Janeczko, Paul B. *Strings: A Gathering of Family Poems*. New York: Bradbury, 1984.

Johnson, James Weldon. *God's Trombones: Seven Negro Sermons in Verse*. Drawings by Aaron Douglass. New York: Viking, 1927. Excellent introduction that discusses the folk sermon. For older boys and girls and adults.

Koch, Kenneth, and Farrell, Kate. *Talking to the Sun: An Illustrated Anthology of Poems for Young People*. New York: Metropolitan Museum of Art and Holt, 1985.

Kuskin, Karla. *Dogs and Dragons, Trees and Dreams: A Collection of Poems*. New York: Harper, 1980.

Larrick, Nancy. *Piping Down the Valleys Wild: Poetry for the Young of All Ages*. Edited, with a new introduction by Nancy Larrick. Illustrated by Ellen Raskin. New York: Delacorte, 1985.

Lewis, Richard. *Miracles: Poems by Children of the English-Speaking World*. New York: Simon & Schuster, 1984.

———. *Out of the Earth I Sing: Poetry and Songs of Primitive Peoples of the Earth*. New York: Norton, 1968, o.p.

Livingston, Myra Cohn. *Cat Poems*. Illustrated by Trina Schart Hyman. New York: Holiday House, 1987.

———. *How Pleasant to Know Mr. Lear! Edward Lear's Selected Works with an Introduction and Notes*. New York: Holiday, 1982.

———. *Worlds I Know and Other Poems*. Drawings by Tim Arnold. New York: Scribner, 1985. Poems that reflect the child's world.

Livingston, Myra Cohn, and Fisher, Leonard Everett. *Celebrations*. New York: Holiday House, 1985. Poems and paintings to mark 16 important days throughout the year, including Martin Luther King Day.

Lobel, Arnold. *The Random House Book of Mother Goose*. New York: Random, 1986.

McCord, David. *One at a Time*. Boston: Little, 1980. Republished 1986. The collected poems of David McCord with a subject index and index of first lines.

Merriam, Eva. *Fresh Paint*. New York: Macmillan, 1986.

Millay, Edna St. Vincent. *Edna St. Vincent Millay's Poems Selected for Young People*. New York: Harper, 1951.

Moore, Lilian. *Something New Begins: New and Selected Poems*. New York: Atheneum, 1982.

Moore, Lilian, and Thurman, Judith. *To See the World Afresh*. New York: Atheneum, 1974.

Morrison, Lillian. *The Break Dance Kids: Poems of Sport, Motion and Locomotion*. New York: Lothrop, 1985.

Oxenbury, Helen. *The Helen Oxenbury Rhyme Book*. Rhymes chosen by Brian Alderson. New York: Morrow, 1986.

Parker, Elinor. *One Hundred Story Poems*. New York: Crowell, 1951.

Plotz, Helen. *Eye's Delight: Poems of Art and Architecture*. New York: Greenwillow, 1983.

————. *Imagination's Other Place: Poems of Science and Mathematics*. New York: Crowell, 1955. Reissued 1987.

Prelutsky, Jack. *Ride a Purple Pelican*. Illustrated by Garth Williams. New York: Greenwillow, 1986. Delightful rhymes for the very young.

Read, Herbert. *This Way Delight*. New York: Pantheon, 1956.

Service, Robert. *The Cremation of Sam McGee*. Paintings by Ted Harrison. New York: Greenwillow, 1987. A classic poem about the gold rush days.

Silverstein, Shel. *Where the Sidewalk Ends*. New York: Harper, 1974.

Stevenson, Robert Louis. *A Child's Garden of Verses*. Illustrated by Michael Foreman. New York: Delacorte, 1985.

Volavkova, H., ed. *I Never Saw Another Butterfly: Children's Drawings and Poems from Theresienstadt Concentration Camp, 1942–1944*. New York: McGraw, 1964, o.p.

Wilner, Isabel. *The Poetry Troupe: An Anthropology of Poems to Read Aloud*. New York: Scribner, 1977.

## Storytelling Recordings

*An Anthology of Negro Poetry for Young People*. Folkways/Scholastic Records, 1958. (7114). Arna Bontemps reads from his anthology *Golden Slippers* (Harper).

*Charlotte's Web*. Pathways of Sound, 1970. (POS 1043). E. B. White reads his book (Harper), chapter by chapter.

*Childe Rowland, and Other British Fairy Tales*. Caedmon, 1969. (TC 1278). Claire Bloom reads five traditional tales from Amabel Williams-Ellis's collection *Fairy Tales from the British Isles* (Warne).

*Cinderella, and Other Fairy Tales*. Caedmon, 1970. (TC 1330). Claire Bloom reads three stories from Walter de la Mare's collection *Tales Told Again* (Knopf).

*Classic Tales from the Picture Book Parade*. Weston Woods, 1986. (WW 734C). Ruth Sawyer reads her version of *Journey Cake, Ho!* The other selections on this tape are "The Three Little Pigs" and "Goldilocks and the Three Bears," narrated by Ian Thomson; "The Elves and the Shoemaker," narrated by Neil Innes; and "The Musicians of Bremen," narrated by Roderick Cook.

*Dick Whittington and His Cat, and Other English Fairy Tales.* Caedmon, 1969. (TC 1265). Claire Bloom reads four English folktales, as retold by James Reeves in his collection *English Fables and Fairy Stories* (Walck).

*Eli Wallach Reads Isaac Bashevis Singer.* Miller-Brody Productions, 1974. (NAR 3063/64). Tales from *Zlateh the Goat and Other Stories* (Harper) and *When Schlemiel Went to Warsaw and Other Stories* (Farrar).

*Elijah's Violin and Other Jewish Fairy Tales.* Pom Records, 1985. (P-1015-16). Peninnah Schram tells three tales from Howard Schwartz's collection: "Elijah's Violin," "The Golden Mountain," and "The Boy Israel and the Witch."

*Ella Jenkins' Nursery Rhymes: Rhyming and Remembering.* Folkways, 1980. (FC 7660). Traditional nursery rhymes sung or read slowly for little childen.

*Elsie Piddock Skips in Her Sleep: Stories and Poems by Eleanor Farjeon.* A Gentle Wind, 1984. (GW 1025). Ellin Greene reads poems by Eleanor Farjeon and tells three Farjeon tales: "Elsie Piddock Skips in Her Sleep," "Nella's Dancing Shoes," and "The Sea-Baby."

*Eva Le Gallienne Reads Hans Christian Andersen.* Miller-Brody Productions, 1973. (L 504-511). Eight of Andersen's best-loved stories.

*An Evening at Cedar Creek.* Wellspring Music, 1987. Side 1: Stories from Indonesia, China and the United States. Side 2: Stories from the Ozarks. Told by Beth Horner, with musical accompaniment.

*Fairy Tale Favorites,* vol. 1. CMS Records, 1970. (CMS 593). Mary Strang tells "Cinderella," "The Sleeping Beauty," and the original French version of "Little Red Riding Hood."

*Fairy Tale Favorites,* vol. 2. CMS Records, 1970. (CMS 595). Mary Strang tells "The Fairies" ("Toads and Diamonds") and three stories by Hans Christian Andersen.

*Fairy Tale Favorites,* vol. 3. CMS Records, 1971. (CMS 632). Mary Strang tells Laurence Housman's "Rocking-Horse Land" and three traditional tales.

*Fairy Tales.* Caedmon, 1963. (TC 1044). Basil Rathbone reads three fairy tales by Oscar Wilde.

*Fairy Tales for a Winter's Night.* CMS Records, 1968. (CMS 534). Mary Strang tells Andersen's "The Fir Tree" and "The Little Match Girl," Grimm's "The Elves and the Shoemaker," and Moore's " 'Twas the Night before Christmas."

*Fairy Tales from the Picture Book Parade.* Weston Woods, 1986. (WW 735C). "Beauty and the Beast," from the book adapted and illustrated by

Warwick Hutton, and "The Ugly Duckling," by Hans Christian Andersen, narrated by Pauline Brailsford; "The Selfish Giant," by Oscar Wilde, narrated by Charles Cioffi; "Red Riding Hood," told in verse by Beatrice Schenk de Regnier and narrated by Carol Birch. With the exception of Red Riding Hood the tellings are accompanied by musical background that is sometimes obtrusive.

*Fairy Tales of Hans Christian Andersen.* Caedmon, 1958. (TC 1073). Michael Redgrave reads four tales, as translated by R. P. Keigwin.

*Favorite Christmas Stories.* CMS Records, 1971. (CMS 629). Mary Strang tells Beatrix Potter's *The Tailor of Gloucester* (Warne) and four other Christmas favorites.

*Folktales from the Picture Book Parade.* Weston Woods, 1981. (WW 717). Includes *A Story—A Story,* by Gail E. Haley, read by Dr. John J. Akar; *Suho and the White Horse,* by Yuzo Otsuka, and *The Great Enormous Turnip,* by Alexei Tolstoy, narrated by Charles Cioff; *Stone Soup,* told by Marcia Brown; and *Arrow to the Sun,* narrated by Gerald McDermott.

*Frances Clarke Sayers, Storyteller.* Weston Woods, 1966. (WW 705, 706). Stories by Carl Sandburg and Hans Christian Andersen.

*The Hairyman and Other Wild Tales.* High Windy Productions, 1981. (IRC 1202). David Holt sings "Groundhog" and tells six stories: "The Hogaphone," "The First Motorcycle in Black Mountain, North Carolina," "Barney McCabe," "The Hairyman," "The Magic Fiddle," and "The Apple Tree," accompanied by banjo, harmonica, fiddle, guitar, and buck dancing. This recording is a good example of the performance type of telling in which different voices are used for different characters. Excellent pacing and relaxed style.

*Hans Christian Andersen in Central Park.* Weston Woods, 1981. (WW 713). Six tales by Hans Christian Andersen: "Hans Clodhopper," "The Goblin and the Grocer," "The Ugly Duckling," "The Emperor's New Clothes," "The Nightingale," and "Dance, Dance, Dolly Mine," as Diane Wolkstein tells them to audiences in Central Park. Pleasing musical accompaniment by Shirley Keller and Wolkstein's daughter, Rachel.

*Honey I Love.* Honey Productions, Inc., 1982. Author Eloise Greenfield and children read poems from her collection. Jazz accompaniment.

*How to Tell Corn Fairies When You See 'Em, and Other Rootabaga Stories,* vol. 2. Caedmon, 1961. (TC 1159). Carl Sandburg tells from his collection *Rootabaga Stories* (Harcourt).

*Jack Tales: More than a Beanstalk.* Weston Woods, 1985. (WW 727). Donald Davis, a native of western North Carolina, tells three Appalachian tales: "Jack and Old Bluebeard," "Jack Tells a Story," and "Jack and the Silver Sword."

*The John Masefield Story-telling Festival.* Toronto Public Library. Highlights from the festivals held in 1961, 1966, 1972 (3 records).

*Joy to the World.* Weston Woods, 1966. (WW 707). Ruth Sawyer tells three stories and a poem from her book of the same title (Little).

*The Little Mermaid.* Caedmon, 1967. (TC 1230). Cathleen Nesbitt reads the Keigwin translation.

*Little Red Riding Hood and the Dancing Princesses.* Caedmon, 1972. (TC 1331). Claire Bloom tells Walter de la Mare's versions from his book *Tales Told Again.*

*Little Wildrose and Other Andrew Lang Fairy Tales.* Caedmon, 1973. (TC 1382). Cathleen Nesbitt reads from Lang's *Crimson Fairy Book* (Dover).

*Nightmares Rising.* Frostfire, 1986. (100). Carol Birch tells four eerie stories: "Mary Culhane and the Dead Man," "Mr. Fox," "The Boy with the Beer Keg," and "Caryn's Story."

*Pearl Primus' Africa.* Miller-Brody Productions, 1971. (P601–3). Traditional legends, folktales, and proverbs of Africa.

*The People Could Fly.* Knopf/Random House, 1987. Twelve tales from *The People Could Fly,* by Virginia Hamilton. Narrated by James Earl Jones and Virginia Hamilton. A Knopf Book and Cassette Classic.

*Perez and Martina.* CMS Records, 1966. (CMS 505). Pura Belpré tells this traditional Puerto Rican folktale in English and Spanish.

*Peter Rabbit and Friends from the Picture Book Parade.* Weston Woods, 1986. (WW 733C). Pauline Brailsford reads five tales by Beatrix Potter: "The Tales of Peter Rabbit," "The Tale of Mr. Jeremy Fisher," "The Tale of Tom Kitten," "The Tale of Benjamin Bunny," and "The Tale of Two Bad Mice." There is no music to distract from the polished readings.

*The Rain God's Daughter and Other African Folktales.* Caedmon, 1970. (TC 1329). Three African tales told by Ruby Dee.

*Richard Chase Tells Three "Jack Tales" from the Southern Appalachians.* Folk Legacy Records, 1963. (FTA-6). The author tells from his collection *The Jack Tales* (Houghton) to a group of children from northeastern Tennessee.

*Rootabaga Stories,* vol. 1. Caedmon, 1966. (TC 1089). vol. 2. Caedmon, 1969. (TC 1306). Told by the author in his slow-moving, rhythmic voice.

*The Seventh Princess, and Other Fairy Tales.* CMS Records, 1968. (CMS 502). Anne Pellowski tells "Cinderella," "The Goose Girl," Eleanor Farjeon's "The Seventh Princess," and Kipling's "The Potted Princess."

*Snow-White and Rose-Red and Other Andrew Lang Fairy Tales.* Caedmon, 1973. (TC 1414). Stories from the *Blue Fairy Book* (Dover) and the *Red Fairy Book* (Peter Smith) told by Glynis Johns.

*The Star Maiden and Other Indian Tales.* CMS Records, 1964. (CMS 500). Anne Pellowski tells four American Indian tales.

*Stories from Many Lands from the Picture Book Parade.* Weston Woods, 1986. (WW 736C). Includes Gerald McDermott narrating his version of *The Stonecutter; The Treasure,* by Uri Shulevitz, narrated by Allen Swift; *Tikki Tikki Tembo,* by Arlene Mosel, narrated by Peter Thomas; *The Hole in the Dike,* by Norma B. Green; and *One Fine Day,* by Nonny Hogrogian, narrated by Emery Battis.

*Stories: Old as the World, Fresh as the Rain.* Weston Woods, 1981. (WW 712). Laura Simms tells stories from Africa and the Far East: "A Single Grain of Rice," "The Woodcutter," "Magoolie," "The Magic Crystal," "Superman," and "The Wooden Box." She is accompanied on this record by her husband, musician Steven Gorn.

*A Story, a Story.* Weston Woods, 1972. (LTR 123). Narrated by John Joseph Akar.

*The Tale of Peter Rabbit.* Caedmon, 1970. (TC 1314). Claire Bloom reads Beatrix Potter's tales of *Peter Rabbit, Benjamin Bunny, Mr. Jeremy Fisher, Mrs. Tiggy-Winkle,* and *Two Bad Mice* (Warne).

*Tales from an Irish Hearth.* The Storytellers School of Toronto, 1985. Alice Kane tells ten traditional Irish tales taken from the works of Patrick Kennedy, T. Crofton Croker, Samuel Lover, and others.

*Tales of the Hopi Indians.* Spoken Arts, 1972. (SA 1106). Told by Diane Wolkstein.

*Tales to Grow On.* Weston Woods, 1981. (WW 711). Side 1: The folktellers tell in tandem "Dark Dark Night," based on the version in *Juba This and Juba That,* by Virginia A. Tashjian, and *The King at the Door,* by Brock Cole, and sing "Mama Mama Have You  Heard" and "Apples and Bananas." Also includes "Sody Sallyraytus," from *Grandfather Tales,* and "Ghost Hunt," told by Connie Regan. Side 2: Barbara Freeman tells "Wicked John and the Devil," from Richard Chase's *Grandfather Tales.* The response of the children in the audience adds to the listener's pleasure.

*Uncle Bouqui of Haiti.* Folkways/Scholastic Records, 1956. (7107). Augusta Baker tells three tales from Harold Courlander's book (Morrow).

*The Velveteen Rabbit.* Miller-Brody Productions, 1976. (L 512). Eva Le Gallienne reads Margery Williams's story (Doubleday).

*Why Mosquitoes Buzz in People's Ears.* Weston Woods, 1976. (LTR 199C). Told by James Earl Jones.

*The Wind in the Willows,* vols. 1–4. Pathways of Sound, 1953. (POS 1022, 1026, 1029, 1030). Chapters from Kenneth Grahame's book of the same name (Scribner) read by Hume Cronyn, Jessica Tandy, and Robert Brooks.

*Zulu and Other African Folktales.* Caedmon, 1975. (TC 1474). Ruby Dee and Ossie Davis tell stories from Verna Aardema's collection *Behind the Back of the Mountain: Black Folktales from Southern Africa* (Dial).

## Storytellers Talk about Storytelling

Augusta Baker. "Storytelling." In *Prelude: Mini-Seminars on Using Books Creatively, Series 1.* New York: Children's Book Council, 1975. Augusta Baker discusses the values of storytelling, the criteria for selection, and the qualities of a good storyteller. She offers hints on preparing and presenting stories to children and tells "Why Crow Is Black and Men Find Precious Stones in the Earth" from *The Earth Is on a Fish's Back: Tales of Beginnings*, by Natalia Belting (Holt). Don Reynolds, a storyteller/librarian, reads from *A Toad for Tuesday*, by Russell E. Erickson (Lothrop), and tells "What Is Trouble?" from *The Knee-High Man and Other Tales*, by Julius Lester (Dial).

Anne Pellowski. "Using Folklore as an Introduction to Other Cultures." In *Prelude: Mini-Seminars on Using Books Creatively, Series 2.* New York: Children's Book Council, 1976. Out of her experience as director of the Information Center on Children's Cultures of the U.S. Committee for UNICEF, Anne Pellowski talks about ways in which folklore can be used to help children learn about other cultures. She describes folkloric programs, combining folktales with music, food, clothing, and/or artifacts, and tells "Eat, My Fine Coat," from *Watermelons, Walnuts and the Wisdom of Allah*, by Barbara Walker (Parents). On the same tape Hewitt Pantaleoni tells "Tweriire" from *Songs and Stories from Uganda*, by Moses Serwadda, translated and edited by Pantaleoni (Crowell).

"Ruth Sawyer, Storyteller." Weston Woods, 1964. (WW 701/702). The renowned storyteller talks about the background of her tales, gives advice to beginning storytellers, and tells four stories: "The Voyage of the Wee Red Cap," from *This Way to Christmas* (Harper), "The Flea," from *Picture Tales from Spain* (Lippincott), "The Peddler of Ballaghadereen," from *The Way of the Storyteller* (Viking), and "A Chinese Fairy Tale," from *Moonshine and Clover* (Jonathan Cape).

# Stories to Tell

## Stories of Special Appeal to Children from Birth to Age 3

*The Baby's Catalogue*, by Janet Ahlberg and Alan Ahlberg. Boston: Little, 1983.

*Brown Bear, Brown Bear, What Do You See?*, by Bill Martin, Jr. Illustrated by Eric Carle. New York: Holt, 1983.

*But Where Is the Green Parrot?*, by Thomas Zacharias. New York: Delacorte, 1978.

*Cat Goes Fiddle-i-Fee*, by Paul Galdone. New York: Clarion, 1985.

*Daddy, Play with Me*, by Shigeo Watanbe. Illustrated by Yasuo Ohtomo. New York: Philomel, 1985. See other titles in this series.

*Dance Away*, by George Shannon. Illustrated by Jose Aruego and Ariane Dewey. New York: Greenwillow, 1982.

*The Elephant and the Bad Baby*, by Elfrida Vipont. Illustrations by Raymond Briggs. New York: Coward, 1969.

*Goodnight Moon*, by Margaret Wise Brown. Illustrated by Clement Hurd. New York: Harper, 1947.

*Good-Night, Owl!*, by Pat Hutchins. New York: Macmillan, 1972.

*Have You Seen My Duckling?*, by Nancy Tafuri. New York: Greenwillow, 1984.

*I Touch*, by Rachel Isadora. New York: Greenwillow, 1985.

*Madeline*, by Ludwig Bemelmans. New York: Viking, 1939.

*May I Bring a Friend?*, by Beatrice Schenk De Regniers. Illustrated by Beni Montresor. New York: Atheneum, 1964.

*Mr. Gumpy's Outing*, by John Burningham. New York: Holt, 1971.

*Over in the Meadow: A Counting Out Rhyme*, by Olie A. Wadsworth. Illustrated by Mary Maki Rae. New York: Viking, 1985.

*Play with Me*, by Marie Hall Ets. New York: Viking, 1955.

*The Snowy Day*, by Ezra Jack Keats. New York: Viking, 1962.

*The Tale of Peter Rabbit*, by Beatrix Potter. New York: Warne, 1902. Reoriginated editions, 1987. See other titles by this author.

*Ten, Nine, Eight*, by Molly Bang. New York: Greenwillow, 1983.

*Umbrella*, by Taro Yashima. New York: Viking, 1958.

*The Very Hungry Caterpillar*, by Eric Carle. New York: World, 1969.

*Welcome, Little Baby*, by Aliki. New York: Greenwillow, 1987.

*When We Went to the Park*, by Shirley Hughes. New York: Lothrop, 1985.

*When You Were a Baby*, by Ann Jonas. New York: Greenwillow, 1982.

*Where's Spot?* by Eric Hill. New York: Putnam, 1980.

## Stories of Special Appeal to 3-to-5-Year-Olds

"The Bed." In *The Tiger and the Rabbit and Other Tales*, by Pura Belpré. Philadelphia: Lippincott, 1965.

"Budulinek." In *The Fairy Tale Treasury*. Selected by Virginia Haviland. New York: Coward, 1972.

*The Elves and the Shoemaker*, by Jakob Grimm and Wilhelm Grimm. Retold by Bernadette Watts. New York: Holt, 1986.

*The Fat Cat: A Danish Folktale*, by Jack Kent. New York: Parents, 1971.

"The Gingerbread Boy." In *The Fairy Tale Treasury*. Selected by Virginia Haviland. New York: Coward, 1972.

*The Great Big Enormous Turnip*, by A. N. Tolstoi. New York: Watts, 1968.

*The Gunniwolf*. Retold by Wilhelmina Harper. New York: Dutton, 1967.

"Henny Penny." In *The Three Bears and 15 Other Stories*, by Anne Rockwell. New York: Crowell, 1975.

*Millions of Cats*, by Wanda Gág. New York: Coward, 1928.

*Mr. and Mrs. Pig's Evening Out*, by Mary Rayner. New York: Macmillan, 1976.

*The Old Woman and Her Pig*, by Paul Galdone. New York: McGraw, 1961.

"Pooh Goes Visiting and Gets into a Tight Place." In *Winnie-the-Pooh*, by A. A. Milne. New York: Dutton, 1926.

"Punia and the King of the Sharks." In *Twenty Tellable Tales*, by Margaret Reed MacDonald. New York: Wilson, 1986.

"Snowflake." In *Picture Tales from the Russian*, by Valery Carrick. Chester Springs, Pa.: Dufour, 1963.

"Star Money." In *The Three Bears and 15 Other Stories*, by Anne Rockwell. New York: Crowell, 1975.

"The Story of the Three Little Pigs." In *English Fairy Tales*, by Joseph Jacobs. New York: Dover, 1898.

"The Sweet Porridge." In *More Tales from Grimm*, by Wanda Gág. New York: Coward, 1947.

*Teeny Tiny*, by Jill Bennett. New York: Putnam, 1986.

"The Three Bears." In *The Golden Goose Book*, by L. Leslie Brooke. New York: Warne, 1905.

*The Three Billy Goats Gruff*, by Peter C. Asbjørnsen and Jørgen E. Moe. New York: Harcourt, 1957.

*What's in Fox's Sack?* Retold by Paul Galdone. New York: Clarion, 1982.

*When the Root Children Wake Up*, by Sibylle von Olfers. Philadelphia: Lippincott, 1941.

*Who's in Rabbit's House?*, by Verna Aardema. New York: Dial, 1977.

*Why the Sun and the Moon Live in the Sky*, by Elphinstone Dayrell. New York: Houghton, 1968.

*The Wolf and the Seven Little Kids*, by Jakob Grimm and Wilhelm Grimm. New York: Harcourt, 1959.

## Stories of Special Appeal to 6-to-8-Year-Olds

"Alligator's Sunday Suit." In *Bo Rabbit Smart for True: Folktales from the Gullah*. Retold by Priscilla Jaquith. New York: Philomel, 1981.

"Baba Yaga and the Little Girl with the Kind Heart." In *Old Peter's Russian Tales*, by Arthur Ransome. Bridgeport, Conn.: Merrimack, 1984.

*The Cat's Purr*, by Ashley Bryan. New York: Atheneum, 1985.

"Cinderella." In *Tales from Grimm*, by Wanda Gág. New York: Coward, 1936.

"The Crab and the Jaguar." In *Picture Folk-Tales*, by Valery Carrick. New York: Dover, 1967.

"The Frog Prince." In *Tales from Grimm*, by Wanda Gág. New York: Coward, 1936.

*Godfather Cat and Mousie*, by Doris Orgel. New York: Macmillan, 1986.

"How to Tell Corn Fairies When You See 'Em." In *Rootabaga Stories*, by Carl Sandburg. New York: Harcourt, 1951.

"I'm Tipingee, She's Tipingee, We're Tippingee, Too." In *The Magic Orange Tree and Other Haitian Folktales*, by Diane Wolkstein. New York: Knopf, 1978.

*Many Moons*, by James Thurber. New York: Harcourt, 1943.

"Mr. Miacca." In *English Fairy Tales*, by Joseph Jacobs. New York: Dover, 1898.

"Molly Whuppie." In *English Folk and Fairy Tales*, by Joseph Jacobs. New York: Putnam, 1904.

"Mother Holle." In *More Tales from Grimm*, by Wanda Gág. New York: Coward, 1947.

*The Old Woman and the Red Pumpkin*, by Betsy Bang. New York: Macmillan, 1975.

"One-Eye, Two-Eyes, and Three-Eyes." In *The Complete Grimm's Fairy Tales*. New York: Pantheon, 1944.

*Perez and Martina*, by Pura Belpré. New York: Warne, 1961.

*Snow-White and the Seven Dwarfs. A Tale from the Brothers Grimm*. Translated by Randall Jarrell. New York: Farrar, 1972.

"Soap, Soap, Soap." In *Grandfather Tales*, by Richard Chase. New York: Houghton, 1948.

"Ti-Jean Brings Home the Moon." In *Tales of the Far North*, by Eva Martin. New York: Dial, 1986.

*Tikki Tikki Tembo*. Retold by Arlene Mosel. New York: Holt, 1968.

"Tom Tit Tot." In *Alan Garner's Book of British Fairy Tales*. New York: Delacorte, 1984.

*The Wedding Procession of the Rag Doll and the Broom Handle and Who Was in It*, by Carl Sandburg. New York: Harcourt, 1967.

"Why the Waves Have Whitecaps." In *The Knee-High Man and Other Tales*, by Julius Lester. New York: Dial, 1972.

"Wiley, His Mama, and the Hairy-Man." In *The People Could Fly: American Black Folktales*, by Virginia Hamilton. New York: Knopf, 1985.

"The Woman Who Flummoxed the Fairies." In *Heather and Broom: Tales of the Scottish Highlands*, by Sorche Nic Leodhas. New York: Holt, 1960.

## Stories of Special Appeal to 8-to-11-Year-Olds

"Anansi's Hat-Shaking Dance." In *The Hat-Shaking Dance and Other Ashanti Tales from Ghana*, by Harold Courlander and Albert K. Prempeh. New York: Harcourt, 1957.

"The Baker's Daughter." In *A Street of Little Shops*, by Margery Bianco. Boston: Grigg, 1981.

"The Boy Israel and the Witch." In *Elijah's Violin and Other Jewish Fairy Tales*. Selected and retold by Howard Schwartz. New York: Harper, 1983.

"The Goat Well." In *The Fire on the Mountain and Other Ethiopian Stories*, by Harold Courlander and Leslau Wolf. New York: Holt, 1950.

"He Lion, Bruh Bear, and Bruh Rabbit." In *The People Could Fly: American Black Folktales*, by Virginia Hamilton. New York: Knopf, 1985.

"How Boots Befooled the King." In *The Wonder Clock*, by Howard Pyle. New York: Dover, 1887, 1915.

"The Hungry Old Witch." In *Tales from Silver Lands*, by Charles J. Finger. New York: Doubleday, 1924.

*John Henry: An American Legend*, by Ezra Jack Keats. New York: Pantheon, 1965.

"King Arthur and His Sword." In *The Story of King Arthur and His Knights*, by Howard Pyle. New York: Scribner, 1903.

*King of the Cats*, by Joseph Jacobs. New York: Clarion, 1980.

"The Magic Ball." In *Tales from Silver Lands*, by Charles J. Finger. New York: Doubleday, 1924.

"Mouse Woman and Porcupine Hunter." In *Mouse Woman and Mischief-Makers*, by Christie Harris. New York: Atheneum, 1977.

"Paul Bunyan. The Winter of the Blue Snow." In *Paul Bunyan Swings His Axe*, by Dell J. McCormick. Caldwell, Idaho: Caxton, 1936.

"The Princess Golden-Hair and the Great Black Raven." In *The Wonder Clock*, by Howard Pyle. New York: Dover, 1887, 1915.

"Rabbit and Coyote." In *The Monkey's Haircut and Other Stories Told by the Maya*. New York: Morrow, 1986.

"The Rat-Catcher's Daughter." In *The Rat-Catcher's Daughter: A Collection of Stories by Laurence Housman*. Selected by Ellin Greene. New York: Atheneum, 1974.

"Robin Hood. The Shooting-Match at Nottingham Town." In *Some Merry Adventures of Robin Hood*, by Howard Pyle. New York: Scribner, 1954.

"The Rooster, the Hand Mill and the Swarm of Hornets." In *The Golden Lynx and Other Tales*. Selected by Augusta Baker. New York: Lippincott, 1960.

"The Snake Brothers," told by Lame Deer. In *The Sound of Flutes, and Other Indian Legends*, by Richard Erdoes. New York: Pantheon, 1976.

"The Talking Stone." In *The Hungry Woman: Myths and Legends of the Aztecs*, by John Bierhorst. New York: Morrow, 1984.

"Ticky-Picky Boom-Boom." In *Anansi, the Spider Man: Jamaican Folk Tales*, by Philip M. Sherlock. New York: Crowell, 1954.

"Turtle Goes Hunting." In *The Naked Bear. Folktales of the Iroquois*. Edited by John Bierhorst. Morrow, 1987.

"Two Giants." In *Tales for the Telling: Irish Folk and Fairy Stories*, by Edna O'Brien. New York: Atheneum, 1986.

"Who Can Break a Bad Habit?" In *African Wonder Tales*, by Frances Carpenter. New York: Doubleday, 1963, o.p. Also in *Twenty Tellable Tales*. New York: Wilson, 1986.

"The Wonderful Brocade." In *The Spring of Butterflies and Other Chinese Folk Tales*, by He Liyi. New York: Lothrop, 1985.


## Stories of Special Appeal to 11-to-15-Year-Olds

"The Boy Pu-nia and the King of the Sharks." In *Legends of Hawaii*, by Padraic Colum. New Haven, Conn.: Yale University Press, 1937.

"Childe Rowland." In *English Fairy Tales*, by Joseph Jacobs. New York: Dover, 1898.

"The Children of Lir." In *A Storyteller's Choice*, by Eileen Colwell. New York: Walck, 1964.

"Clever Manka." In *The Shepherd's Nosegay*, by Parker Fillmore. Edited by Katherine Love. New York: Harcourt, 1958.

"The Cow-Tail Switch." In *The Cow-Tail Switch and Other West African Stories*, by Harold Courlander and George Herzog. New York: Holt, 1947.

"Cupid and Psyche." In *Greek Myths*, by Olivia Coolidge. New York: Houghton, 1949.

"Finn and the Snakes." In *The Green Hero: Early Adventures of Finn Mc-Cool*, by Bernard Evslin. New York: Four Winds, 1975.

"Ghost Canoe People." In *The Trouble with Adventurers*, by Christie Harris. New York: Atheneum, 1982.

"The Girl Who Cried Flowers." In *The Girl Who Cried Flowers and Other Tales*, by Jane Yolen. New York: Crowell, 1974.

"Kate Crackernuts." In *Alan Garner's Book of British Fairy Tales*, by Alan Garner. New York: Delacorte, 1984.

"The Lass That Couldn't Be Frighted." In *Heather and Broom: Tales of the Scottish Highlands*, by Sorche Nic Leodhas. New York: Holt, 1960.

"Mr. Fox." In *Ardizzone's English Fairy Tales: Twelve Classic Tales*. Selected and illustrated by Edward Ardizzone. Taken from the collections of Joseph Jacobs. London: Deutsch, 1980.

"The Nightingale and the Rose." In *The Happy Prince and Other Stories*. London: Dent, 1977.

"The Return of Odysseus." In *The Adventures of Odysseus*, by Padraic Colum. New York: Macmillan, 1918. Also in *Hero Tales from Many Lands*, by Alice I. Hazeltine. Nashville: Abingdon, 1961.

"Shrewd Todie and Lyzer the Miser." In *When Shlemiel Went to Warsaw and Other Stories*, by Isaac B. Singer. New York: Farrar, 1968.

"The Snowman." In *Hans Christian Andersen: The Complete Fairy Tales & Stories*. Translated from the Danish by Erik C. Haugaard. New York: Doubleday, 1974.

"The Story of Washing Horse Pond." In *The Spring of Butterflies and Other Chinese Folktales*, by He Liyi. New York: Lothrop, 1985.

"The Tell-Tale Heart." In *The Pit and the Pendulum and Five Other Tales*, by Edgar Allan Poe. New York: Watts, 1967.

*Tristan and Iseult*, by Rosemary Sutcliff. New York: Dutton, 1971. (Tell as a cycle story, or read aloud a few chapters at a sitting.)

"The Very Pretty Lady." In *The Devil's Storybook*, by Natalie Babbitt. New York: Farrar, 1974.

"White Bear Whittington." In *Grandfather Tales*, by Richard Chase. Boston: Houghton, 1948.

"Wicked John and the Devil." In *Grandfather Tales*, by Richard Chase. New York: Houghton, 1948.

"The Woodcutter of Gura." In *The Fire on the Mountain and Other Ethiopian Stories*, by Harold Courlander. New York: Holt, 1950.

"The Wooing of the Maze." In *The Rat-Catcher's Daughter: A Collection of Stories by Laurence Housman*. Selected by Ellin Greene. New York: Atheneum, 1974.

"A Young Prince Named Siegfried." In *The Story of Siegfried*, by James Baldwin. New York: Scribner, 1931.

## Stories of Special Appeal to a Mixed-Age Group

*Aladdin and the Wonderful Lamp,* by Andrew Lang. New York: Viking, 1981.

"Billy Beg and the Bull" and "The Cat and the Parrot." In *The Lost Half-Hour.* Edited by Eulalie S. Ross. New York: Harcourt, 1963.

"The Elephant's Child." In *Just So Stories,* by Rudyard Kipling. New York: Holt, 1987.

*The Foolish Frog,* by Pete Seeger and Charles L. Seeger. New York: Macmillan, 1973.

"The Huckabuck Family and How They Raised Pop Corn in Nebraska and Quit and Came Back." In *Rootabaga Stories,* by Carl Sandburg. New York: Harcourt, 1923.

"Jack and the Beanstalk." In *Ardizzone's English Fairy Tales: Twelve Classic Tales.* Selected and illustrated by Edward Ardizzone. Taken from the collection of Joseph Jacobs. London: Deutsch, 1980.

"The King with the Terrible Temper." In *With a Deep Sea Smile,* by Virginia A. Tashjian. Boston: Little, 1974.

"Kuratko the Terrible." In *The Shepherd's Nosegay,* by Parker Fillmore. Edited by Katherine Love. New York: Harcourt, 1958.

"The Little Rooster and the Turkish Sultan." In *The Good Master,* by Kate Seredy. New York: Viking, 1935.

"Mr. Sampson Cat." In *Picture Tales from the Russian,* by Valery Carrick. Chester Springs, Pa.: Dufour, 1963.

*The Month Brothers: A Slavic Tale,* by Samuel Marshak. New York: Morrow, 1983.

"Peterkin and the Little Grey Hare." In *The Wonder Clock,* by Howard Pyle. New York: Harper, 1887, 1915.

*Rapunzel,* by Jakob and Wilhelm Grimm. New York: Harcourt, 1966.

"Rikki-Tikki-Tavi." In *The Jungle Book,* by Rudyard Kipling. New York: Doubleday, 1932.

"The Selfish Giant." In *The Birthday of the Infants and Other Tales,* by Oscar Wilde. New York: Atheneum, 1982.

*The Seven Ravens,* by Jakob and Wilhelm Grimm. New York: Harcourt, 1963.

"The Seventh Princess." In *The Little Bookroom,* by Eleanor Farjeon. New York: Godine, 1984.

"Sody Sallyraytus." In *Grandfather Tales,* by Richard Chase. New York: Houghton, 1948.

*Stone Soup,* by Marcia Brown. New York: Scribner, 1947.

*A Story, a Story: An African Tale,* by Gail Haley. New York: Atheneum, 1970.

*The Story of Persephone,* by Penelope Farmer. New York: Morrow, 1973.

"The Three Sillies." In *Ardizzone's English Fairy Tales: Twelve Classic Tales.* Selected and illustrated by Edward Ardizzone. Taken from the collection of Joseph Jacobs. London: Deutsch, 1980.

"The Ugly Duckling." In *It's Perfectly True and Other Stories,* by Hans Christian Andersen. New York: Harcourt, 1938.

"Uncle Bouqui and Godfather Ti-Malice." In *Uncle Bouqui of Haiti,* by Harold Courlander. New York: Morrow, 1942.

"Why Dogs Hate Cats." In *the Knee-High Man and Other Tales,* by Julius Lester. New York: Dial, 1972.

## Stories of Special Appeal for the Family Story Hour

"The Buried Moon." In *The Buried Moon and Other Stories.* Selected by Molly Bang. New York: Scribner, 1977.

"Cap O'Rushes." In *Ardizzone's English Fairy Tales: Twelve Classic Tales.* Selected and illustrated by Edward Ardizzone. Taken from the collection of Joseph Jacobs. London: Deutsch, 1980.

*The Dancing Granny,* by Ashley Bryan. New York: Atheneum, 1977.

"Dulce Domum." In *The Wind in the Willows,* by Kenneth Grahame. New York: Scribner, 1908.

"Elsie Piddock Skips in Her Sleep." In *Martin Pippin in the Daisy Field,* by Eleanor Farjeon. Philadelphia: Lippincott, 1937.

"Eshu." In *Orisha: The Gods of Yorubaland,* by Judith Gleason. New York: Atheneum, 1971.

*Gone Is Gone,* by Wanda Gág. New York: Coward, 1935.

"Gubrand-on-the-Hillside." In *East of the Sun and West of the Moon.* New York: Viking, 1969.

"How the Moonfish Came to Be." In *Greedy Mariani and Other Folktales of the Antilles,* by Dorothy S. Carter. New York: Atheneum, 1974.

"It's Perfectly True." In *It's Perfectly True and Other Stories,* by Hans Christian Andersen. New York: Harcourt, 1938.

"Kaleeba." In *Songs and Stories from Uganda,* by W. Moses Serwadda. New York: Crowell, 1974.

*The Little Juggler,* by Barbara Cooney. New York: Hastings, 1961.

"A Lover of Beauty." In *Greek Myths,* by Olivia Coolidge. New York: Houghton, 1949.

"The Mixed-Up Feet and the Silly Bridegroom." In *Zlateh the Goat and Other Stories*, by Isaac B. Singer. New York: Harper, 1966.

"Oranges and Lemons." In *Italian Peepshow*, by Eleanor Farjeon. Palo Alto, Calif.: Stokes, 1926.

"The Palace on the Rock." In *The Wonder Dog: The Collected Stories of Richard Hughes*. New York: Morrow, 1977.

"The Sleeping Beauty." In *Told under the Green Umbrella*, by the Literature Committee of the Association for Childhood Education International. New York: Macmillan, 1935.

"Three Boys with Jugs of Molasses and Secret Ambitions." In *Rootabaga Stories*, by Carl Sandburg. New York: Harcourt, 1951.

"Three Strong Women." In *The Woman in the Moon and Other Forgotten Heroines*, by James Riorden. New York: Dial, 1985.

"Two of Everything." In *The Magic Umbrella and Other Stories for Telling*. Chosen and annotated by Eileen Colwell. London: Bodley Head, 1976.

"Uncle Bouqui Rents a Horse." In *Uncle Bouqui of Haiti*, by Harold Courlander. New York: Morrow, 1942.

"The Voyage of the Wee Red Cap." In *This Way to Christmas*, by Ruth Sawyer. New York: Harper, 1967.

"What Is Trouble?" In *The Knee-High Man and Other Tales*, by Julius Lester. New York: Dial, 1972.

*Why the Sky Is Far Away: A Folktale from Nigeria*. Retold by Mary-Joan Gerson. New York: Harcourt, 1974.

"Yellow Ribbon." In *The Rainbow Book of American Folk Tales and Legends*, by Maria Leach. New York: World, 1958.

# Appendix 3
# Glossary

Cumulative tale: A repetitive tale characterized by minimum plot and maximum rhythm, e.g., "The Gingerbread Boy."

Droll: A story about sillies or numbskulls, e.g., *The Wise Men of Helm and Their Merry Tales*, by Solomon Simon (Behrman House).

Epic: A cycle of tales centered around one hero, e.g., *The Green Hero: Early Adventures of Finn McCool*, by Bernard Evslin (Four Winds).

Fable: A brief story that teaches a moral lesson; usually the main characters are animals that speak as humans, e.g., Aesop's fables.

Fairy tale: A story involving the "little people": fairies, elves, pixies, gnomes, dwarfs, brownies, leprechauns, e.g., "The Woman Who Flummoxed the Fairies."

Folktale: A traditional story in which quite ordinary people have extraordinary adventures involving magical objects, transformations, talking animals, e.g., "East o' the Sun and West o' the Moon."

Hero tale: A tale that recounts the exploits of a human hero who embodies the ideals of a culture, e.g., *The Story of King Arthur and His Knights*, by Howard Pyle (Scribner).

Legend: Narrative about a person, place, or event involving real or pretended belief, e.g., "The Legend of the Palm Tree."

Literary fairy tale: A story that uses the form of the traditional folktale or fairy tale but that has an identifiable author, e.g., the stories of Eleanor Farjeon.

Motif: The smallest element that persists in a traditional tale, e.g., the favorite youngest child.

Myth: A story about the gods, demigods, or culture heroes that attempts to explain natural phenomena or the origins of human civilization and customs, e.g., "Pandora's Box."

Realistic story: A story that is true to life. It may be a biography, a historical novel, an adventure tale, or an animal story, e.g., *Julie of the Wolves*, by Jean George (Harper).

Religious tale: A story that uses elements of religious belief, e.g., "The Juggler of Notre Dame."

Romance: A medieval story in verse or prose based on chivalrous love and adventure, e.g., *The Story of Roland*, by James Baldwin (Scribner).

Talking animal tale: A story that teaches a moral lesson but so subtly that we are not aware of it, e.g., the African Wakaima and Anansi stories. The main character(s) are animals.

Tall tale: Exaggerated stories about extraordinary persons or animals, e.g., "Pecos Bill Becomes a Coyote."

Traditional tale: A story that has been handed down from one generation to another, either by writing or by word of mouth. There is no identifiable author.

Type: A recognizable tale for which variants are known.

Variant: A different version of the same tale, e.g., "Tom Tit Tot" is the English version of the German "Rumpelstiltskin."

# Index